T0068142

"Perfect for anyone in sales to read to refresh or start a career in selling."
"Like Tim I started in food service and this eventually led me to a sales career. This book was a needed refresher and a tool to help my new sales department recruits who need the moral support of a mentor and the drive of successful leaders. Easy and brief read for any sales professional new or seasoned."

"I love everything about this book."
"I loved everything about this book: thoughtful business/life insights and constructive/applicable suggestions, coupled with light humor and an easily digestible (non-dense) writing style.

More specifically, I deeply resonated with ALL of the messages and insights Tim discusses in Passionate Ambivalence--such as finding a job/service that you are proud to represent and "sell". In fact, the recommendations he offers in the book, helped lead me to find my dream job! I also thoroughly enjoyed the constructive "homework" assignments and refer to them on a daily basis.

As evidence of my high praise, I shared this book with my company and have recommended the assignments and messages to them as well--which has been a great positive impact to our work culture/philosophy. If you want to establish a great work/life philosophy to guide you as you do your business--this is one of the most useful and enjoyable books you could hope to come across"

"Five stars!"
"Anyone would benefit from reading this book, but especially if you are in client care!"

"Start with the basics and succeed."
"Thanks to Tim Clairmont for sharing his new book "Passionate
Ambivalence." Great read on the basics of ethical sales and
service with some great life philosophy for good measure.

Highly recommended for sales managers and new salespeople
alike who want to make sure they know the basics. The lessons
Tim shares in this book have made me millions in sales."

"A required read!"
"My office manager said it best when she said ... Passionate Ambivalence,
would be a required read for anyone that worked for her, had she
known about the book in her Allstate home office days. She quantifies
your program as taking off 10 years of the learning curve to achieve
success in our business, personally and professionally. She started
out skeptical about everything and has since come to profoundly
respect [Tim] and [Tim's] ideas independent of my input."

PASSIONATE AMBIVALENCE

How to Sell with Authenticity and Integrity

Tim Clairmont

PASSIONATE AMBIVALENCE
HOW TO SELL WITH AUTHENTICITY AND INTEGRITY

Securities are offered through ClearFP Securities, LLC, member FINRA & SIPC. Investment Advisory Services are offered through ClearFP Advisors, LLC. ClearFP Securities, LLC and ClearFP Advisors, LLC are wholly owned subsidiaries of Clear Financial Partners, Inc.

The information, ideas, and suggestions in this book are not intended to render professional advice. Before following any suggestions contained in this book, you should consult your personal accountant or other financial advisor. Neither the author nor the publisher shall be liable or responsible for any loss or damage allegedly arising as a consequence of your use or application of any information or suggestions in this book.

iUniverse books may be ordered through booksellers or by contacting:

iUniverse
1663 Liberty Drive
Bloomington, IN 47403
www.iuniverse.com
844-349-9409

Because of the dynamic nature of the Internet, any web addresses or links contained in this book may have changed since publication and may no longer be valid. The views expressed in this work are solely those of the author and do not necessarily reflect the views of the publisher, and the publisher hereby disclaims any responsibility for them.

Any people depicted in stock imagery provided by Getty Images are models, and such images are being used for illustrative purposes only. Certain stock imagery © Getty Images.

ISBN: 978-1-6632-5517-4 (sc)
ISBN: 978-1-6632-5518-1 (e)

Library of Congress Control Number: 2023914581

Print information available on the last page.

iUniverse rev. date: 12/21/2023

Contents

Contents

Dedicated to my mom, Shelley, who taught me to respect
and love *everyone*, and my dad, Dennis, who taught me
the virtues of honesty, self-discipline, paying attention to
the details, and following through on your word.

And, to my wife, Crystal,
Your inspiration, insight, and resolve have been a lesson to us all.
And, your fire has shown me the meaning of the word Passionate.

I Love You

Note to the Reader

When I first started writing this book I typed an introduction trying to explain why everyone should read it. I wanted to let all the salespeople of the world know why they should care about their customers, and I wanted to convince them that the top salespeople are the ones who care about their customers the most.

While I still believe that this is true, I don't know it for sure. Regardless, I *can* say with confidence that this book is *not* for salespeople who don't care about their customers. If you don't care about your customers, please don't read any further. In fact, if you don't care about your customers, please consider a different career. It's people like you who stay in sales for the wrong reasons that give salespeople a bad reputation.

If you do care about your customers, then this book is about how you can show them that you care *even more*. This is about how you can help them in their own personal journey toward happiness.

The old-school ways of selling where you try to manipulate and cajole your prospective client into buying something are truly obsolete. We live in a time when people have endless information at their fingertips. They care what you think, but they know much of the basic information themselves. Most of all, they want a salesperson they can trust. If you are looking for more manipulative sales tactics to figure out how to take advantage of more people and "close more sales," then please don't continue to read this book.

If you are interested in helping to promote what I believe to be one of the most noble professions on the planet, that of an ethical salesperson, then please read further. And, *share* what you read. I want *everyone* to be happier. That is why I wake up each morning. That is why I run my wealth management firm. That is why I wrote this book. I hope that is why you are reading it.

Introduction

I have a shocking revelation for you: Salespeople don't just sell used cars. I know; it's crazy, right?

Consider this: If you have ever waited tables, then you were in sales. If you have ever worked a concession stand at a movie theater or a cash register at a fast food restaurant, then you were in sales. If you ever worked with customers in any kind of retail store (Nordstrom, Target, Cabela's, Walmart, Safeway, and all the other stores we shop at every day), then you were in sales. If you have ever provided a *service* to any customers as a profession (hairstylist, nail expert, car mechanic, accountant, lawyer, cosmetic surgeon and so many more), then you were in sales. And, if you have ever owned any kind of a successful business, then you *know* that you were in sales.

Most of the people we know have been, at some point in their lives, in a position of selling something. Whether it was running a garage sale, listing a car on Craig's List, or volunteering to run a student store or concession stand at a kids' sports game, they have been in sales. But that's "them," right? Not you? Wait a minute...if "they've" been in sales, then maybe "you've" been in sales too...?

Okay, so you finally admitted that you are (or at least at some point in your life *were*) in sales. I know. It was probably hard to do. It's not like your parents raised you with some encouraging "go get 'em" attitude while bragging to their friends about how their son or daughter was going to be an amazing salesperson. It's not like your guidance counselor sat you down and said, "What you want to do is to pursue a college-bound track where you will have an amazing career as a professional salesperson."

It's not like all those TV shows that you watched as a kid portrayed how great life would be if you could only get a job in…sales.

No, most likely your parents and guidance counselors were like mine. They echoed the societal belief that the sure way to happiness and success was to pursue an exciting career as a doctor or a lawyer. Your high school guidance counselor probably compared your academic scores to the admission averages for the best college where you would most likely be admitted. Then, if you had a good academic record, they would encourage you to pursue your goals, go to college, and probably become a doctor or a lawyer. If you had a bad academic record, then they probably told you to pursue your goals and go to college hoping that things might "click" for you later and you could then become a doctor or a lawyer.

After watching TV shows like *ER*, *L.A. Law* or *Law and Order*, your parents probably examined your report cards and encouraged you to go to college and become a…you guessed it…a *doctor* or a *lawyer*.

Society just doesn't give a lot of respect to the profession of *salesperson*.

When most people think of a salesperson, the classic "used car salesman" image usually comes to mind. What does that look like? The stereotypical "used car salesman" is a cliché, disingenuous, manipulator who is willing to lie, cheat and steal his way into making as much money as possible. This swindler takes advantage of the helpless purchaser by selling them something that they don't want, don't need, and/or something that is worthless immediately after purchase.

Furthermore, embracing their absolute lack of morals, this corrupt individual will go home and brag to their friends and family about how they took advantage of some poor schmuck who was foolish enough to work with them in the first place.

No *wonder* so many people hate shopping for a car.

I'm going to ask you a question: Do you really think that all car salesmen are like this?

I'm betting that you answered that question with a "no," but you still most likely aren't eager to go out and shop for a used car today. This stereotype still scares many of us away from the lots. In fact, thanks to this handful of unethical salespeople, we now have tremendous skepticism whenever we approach *any* kind of salesperson.

Conquering our own fears of the potential shame that our friends and family might bestow upon us if we get a "bad deal," we approach these salespeople like we are going into battle. Some of us act as timid warriors. We approach nervous and afraid, worried that we will get that bad deal. Others prepare for battle. We invest lots of time researching our purchase beforehand on the Internet or in magazines.

Then, armed with the knowledge we have obtained, we walk into battle hoping to have a better chance at winning the war. Still others approach the salesperson with confidence or even arrogance. We hold on to our belief in our ability to win against this vile salesperson's manipulative tactics. Finally, many of us decide instead to turn away from that battle. With our tails between our legs, we conclude that we don't really need that product or service after all. We trudge away defeated. With a feigned sense of pride, we tell anyone who asks that we decided to drive that beat-up old car for "one more year." The reality – we just didn't want to deal with the "hassle" (salesperson) of replacing it.

Now let me ask you another question: *Who* would want to be a salesperson with this kind of stereotype? I'm serious. It's a wonder we have any salespeople in this world at all.

Let me give you another scenario. You are having a pleasant conversation with someone you have just met. You have things in common. You are starting to like them. You feel like they are starting to like you. You ask them what they do for a living. They tell you that they are in some form of sales. In fact, they might be able to help you by selling you something. How do you feel? Hurt? Betrayed? Cautious? Concerned?

Even though you, yourself, might *have* some kind of a career in sales, you *still* probably experience some version of these emotions.

These are common emotions that many of us are trained to feel when we encounter someone in sales. We question the authenticity of everything we were feeling up to the point when we found out this person was in sales. We question and reevaluate this person's integrity. Can we trust them?

I believe real salespeople today are acting in one of the noblest of all professions. The basic job of a salesperson is to assist an interested buyer in the acquisition of the best product or service that will help them the most. In other words: **Your job as a salesperson is to help other people be happier.** In today's society, what could be more satisfying than helping other people be happy?

Our country was founded on the belief that all people are created equal and that every citizen has the right to life, liberty, and the pursuit of happiness. Thanks to the abundance of food, shelter, and competent medical providers, most of us in this country don't need much help on a daily basis to survive. Thanks to the sacrifices of our veterans and the currently active members of the armed forces, we don't need much help in our everyday lives to maintain our freedom. But, all of us could use some help from our friends, family, and neighbors in our individual pursuits of happiness.

Most everyone would agree that a doctor and a soldier are serving us in a noble profession. A doctor is required to put their patient's interests above their own as they heal the sick and save lives. Our armed forces put their lives on the line every day to defend our freedom. I believe that there is no better person than an ethical salesperson, who puts their customers' interests above their own, to assist us in our pursuit of happiness.

For all of you brave people out there who have decided to make a career for yourselves in sales, I am writing this book for you.

PART 1

THE BASICS

Chapter 1

No Respect, No Respect

Rodney Dangerfield coined this phrase in many movies and stand-up comic routines, and I find no four words that better describe the biggest challenge to being an ethical salesperson. In so many ways this lack of respect is truly unfortunate.

Ethical salespeople fight the "used car salesman" stereotype every day. Though they may be shunned by their new acquaintances and questioned by their oldest friends, they still stand tall amidst this scrutiny while they help their customers in the best way that they know how.

This challenge creates significant drawbacks with regard to image. In fact, most salespeople will never even admit they are in sales. They search for any other way to introduce themselves to strangers. They craft and practice their elevator speeches to pique interest, captivate a prospect, and avoid giving any friend, family member, or new acquaintance a premature signal that they might be in sales.

Many of the titles of certain professions are even reworked to avoid the implication of sales. Realtors are now Real Estate Professionals. Entrepreneurs are now Founders. Financial Planners are now Wealth Managers. Sales Clerks are now Shoe Professionals, Wardrobe Assistants, and Cosmetic Experts. With so much careful wordsmithing that must be done to achieve success despite the stereotypes, it is no wonder that people continue to question salespeople's motives.

Grabbing and holding your prospect's attention without scaring them away is similar to fishing. One of the most successful means of fishing is

1

to design a fly or carefully place bait so that you simultaneously attract fish and conceal the hook. Next, you cast your line in a place where a fish is likely to discover your lure or your bait. Finally, the fish grabs the bait, and the fisherman reels in the catch. *Unlike* the fish that gets hooked and eaten, however, the customer in a sales transaction *receives something that benefits them.*

In this no-respect environment, a jaded salesperson can easily forget the benefits that they bring to their fish. After being treated like a fisherman who is trying to *hook their catch,* they eventually start to *believe* that they *are* that wicked fisherman. Slipping into that role, they turn their focus on catching fish, and they forget the value that they bring to the fish in the first place. When you believe that the rest of the world has no respect for you, it is sometimes hard to remember to have respect for the rest of the people in the world. While this environment makes the job of a salesperson harder, this lack of respect can be a huge advantage to the income of a salesperson.

You see, there is one universal law that I have noticed over the years: **the world rewards people who are either *capable* of doing what others *cannot, willing* to do what others *will* not, or both.** To arrive at this conclusion I have to thank my high school economics teacher who said it so simply and clearly: "Everything is about supply and demand."

For those of you who understand supply and demand already, you can skip this paragraph. But, for those of you who are new to this concept (or who would like a quick refresher), then let me break it down for you. The economic theory goes like this: The relationship between the supply of any product or service and the demand for that product or service will ultimately determine the price. For example, when Christmas time is upon us, the *demand* usually goes up for the best/hottest present of the year. By Thanksgiving, that item is usually very hard to come by at the stores – the *supply* is low. Therefore, you can usually find some entrepreneurial "friends" who were wise enough to buy up some of the supply early and sell it online for a generous markup just in time for you to get that present for your child before the December 25th cutoff – the *price* goes up. Some people sell things like this every year to make extra money for the holidays. Though many of us may pay that premium for the newest toy and look at it as the price of procrastination, it is really all about supply and demand.

Side Note: (My favorite holiday movie is *Jingle All The Way* with Arnold Schwarzenegger. If you want to watch a fun movie that illustrates *supply and demand*, this is a great one to check out.)

When we apply the rule of *supply and demand* to various careers we find that the *supply* of people willing and capable of performing a job and the *demand* by society for people to perform that job determine the *price* that society is willing to pay for that performance. That *price* is reflected in the form of income.

Think about it. Professional athletes are often idolized for their huge paychecks and worldwide fame and respect. Why are they paid so much? There are plenty of people *willing* to be professional athletes, but there is a low *supply* of people who are *capable* of performing at the highest levels. There is a huge *demand* for us to be entertained by watching these athletes do things that most of us wish we were capable of doing. (Think about how much money we all spend on sporting events, memorabilia, etc.) There are a limited number of spots on the teams that we all like to watch, and there are only a handful of athletes in the world who can qualify for those spots. The *demand* is high. The *supply* is low. Therefore, the *price* that we are willing to pay is very high in the form of huge incomes.

3

Now, look at teachers. This group of workers is widely agreed on as being one of the most underappreciated and underpaid classes of employees in our society today. Why? Teachers have great hours, and their profession comes with tremendous respect. Lots of people can raise their own children while they teach without sacrificing much time away from their kids. (The work hours and time off usually coincide closely with the time that the kids are in and out of school.) Furthermore, most of the teachers are government employees who receive pretty great health benefits and pretty decent pensions when they retire. Therefore, there are a lot more people *willing* to take this job. The *supply* of willing and capable teachers for this job is greater than the *demand* for teachers to do this job. This pushes the *price* down for the average teacher in the form of a lower income.

Some of the things that affect the *supply* of people who are willing and capable of performing a job are: work hours, respect/appreciation for that profession, time off, fringe benefits, fame, and the difficulty to perform the duties of that profession. Things that affect the *demand* for a profession are determined by the needs of society at the moment.

Thanks to the universal desire to maintain our health, there will always be a steady *demand* for quality healthcare (doctors, nurses, etc.) Thanks to our litigious society and our mountains of legislation, there will also be a steady *demand* for legal experts to interpret, prosecute, and defend our actions inside or outside of a courtroom. Maybe this is why our parents and guidance counselors have been pushing us toward these careers for so many years. They have somehow tapped into the dependable nature of these professions, and every parent wants their child to be successful (or at least employed.)

One of the strongest societal trends right now is its *demand* for some form of entertainment. Whether it is in the form of television content, movies, sporting events, video games, phone/tablet applications, or any other product that might make our lives more enjoyable, there is a huge increase in the *demand* for quality entertainment. The *price* for the quality performance of these jobs is reflected in the incomes that these workers receive.

Most of the other underappreciated and underpaid classes of workers in our society can be easily understood through this same theory. Firefighters, police officers, our members of the armed services—these professions all come with a high degree of respect. Thanks to pretty efficient fire planning and excellent systems for protecting us from criminals, the *demand* for firefighters and police officers has decreased in recent years. Due largely to the respect given to the people in these professions, the number of people willing to perform these tasks is rather high. Therefore, with the *supply* of people willing to perform these jobs high, and the *demand* for the people needed for these jobs low, the income is often lower than many feel is fair.

The sales profession is one of the most highly paid professions in our country. A statistic was shared with me after I graduated college in 1997 that over 90 percent of the country's six-figure income earners achieved their incomes through sales. Less than 10 percent were from doctors, lawyers, corporate executives, athletes, etc. I don't know what the statistics are for high-income earners now, but I suspect that the overwhelming majority of income earners over $300,000 per year are likely in some form of sales or sales management.

Chapter 2

The Significance of Trust

There are many factors that will have a huge effect on the success of any transaction between a salesperson and a customer. If you ask a customer why they purchased from a particular salesperson you will get a variety of answers like these: - They knew exactly what I needed. - They really understood the details. - They always know what I want. - I like them. - They explained things well. - They took the time to listen to me. - I would have bought it from anyone. I just wanted the product, and I dealt with the first salesperson I met.

It may seem overwhelming to look for the commonalities among these comments, but there is an underlying thread throughout all of the reasons why a sale goes through – *trust*.

A minimum level of trust must be reached before any client will choose to do business with a salesperson. No one will do business with you unless they have at least some level of trust in you, your product, or your service.

Brand recognition is all about creating an image that people can trust. Think about any brand that you might like: Apple, Mercedes, BMW, Coca-Cola, Pepsi, Costco etc. The list continues. Each one of these companies has created a brand that gives their consumers confidence. Their consumers have to trust the quality of these products, the company's return policy, the service standards, the ethical standards, and so many other features that give customers the confidence to go out and buy from these companies.

Often, the level of trust is so high in some brands that consumers will simply purchase their products without any further help from a salesperson. They will buy them online themselves or walk into a store and buy them off the shelves.

When is the last time that you saw a salesperson get paid a commission to sell you a can of Coca-Cola at a grocery store? Imagine the first person who ever drank a Coca-Cola. "Hey, here is a dark, bubbling, sweet liquid that tastes good. Why don't you drink some?" Do you think that first drinker of Coca-Cola had to trust the salesperson encouraging him or her to drink it? When a brand reaches a certain trust level, the company doesn't need to spend money paying salespeople to sell one can at a time.

Some stores have salespeople out of habit, and even bad salespeople might get paid commissions to sell good products. Having a high degree of trust between the customer and the product being sold has huge cost savings and expansion benefits. How does that brand recognition translate in the service industry?

Some companies have built a successful brand that is based on providing quality service, but most of our service professionals have clients because the person providing the service is **trusted.** Too many service professionals (salespeople) have ignored the many benefits of being trusted. The biggest of these benefits is **saving time**.

In the service industry, time is money. If it takes you twice as long to provide your service to one person for the same price as someone else, then you could have earned twice the revenue and helped twice as many people by providing that service faster.

For example, let's assume that Judy is a hairstylist who charges $50 for a haircut that takes 30 minutes at the best possible quality that she can provide. Now, a customer walks into Judy's store, and she doesn't trust her. That customer takes 5-10 minutes of Judy's time trying to explain the style, look at pictures, verify that Judy knows what she's doing, and maybe asks Judy to show some examples of work she has done. After sitting down, the customer continues to question Judy's choices throughout the haircut, and, by the time Judy is finished, the whole process has taken 60 minutes. If this customer had trusted Judy enough to just walk in, sit down, and let Judy do what she does best, then Judy could have helped two customers in the same amount of time. This is basic math, but I see service professionals (salespeople) forget these basics *all the time!*

There are all kinds of excuses that a salesperson can make at this point. As you read the simple example above you may have caught yourself making these kinds of excuses. If you started thinking these kinds of thoughts in your head, then I encourage you to write them down on a sheet of paper: - I need more time for some people than others. - Quality is important, and I won't be rushed to sacrifice the quality of what my customers are receiving. - Well, the first interview with a customer always takes longer as you build trust. It goes faster later. There are many, many more. I assure you; I have heard them all.

Now that you are done writing down the excuses, let me address them. I get it. I really do. You *can't* sacrifice quality. You *do* have to spend time building trust. Some people *do* take more time than others. I am not here to judge how you do your business. Maybe you are already as efficient as you can possibly be.

What I am saying is this: *Very few people like trying to convince a client to trust them. So, don't waste any more time than necessary doing that.* Nobody likes having to prove themselves to their new customer. I don't know any salesperson that likes having their integrity or the quality of their work doubted. Sure, some people are oblivious to the customer's doubt. These salespeople think that a customer is just asking about how they provide their services and who they have provided them for because they are interested in knowing more about the service and/or the people you have performed your services for. WRONG. These questions are specifically for the purpose of building a level of trust that is high enough for this customer to decide whether or not they will do business with you.

A high trust level means you can spend less time convincing people to trust you and more time helping more people. If you like visiting with certain clients more than others, that's fine. Go buy them a drink after work with the extra money that you earned by taking care of them faster. Or, ask them if they ever talk about your services. Would they maybe be willing to send more people your way? This can save you time that you would otherwise spend marketing. Any time saved can be spent helping more people, being with your family, or having some alone/recharge time... Or, *enjoy* taking the extra time and recognize it for what it is.

As you move forward in your relationships with your clients, make a conscious effort to look at what you spend your time doing. Everything that you *do*, *don't do*, *say*, or *don't say* is making a deposit or taking a withdrawal from your client's Trust Bank. If you aren't sure if certain things are making a deposit or taking a withdrawal, then *ask* your best clients. They already like you, and they will tell you why they do business with you. You might be surprised at the things they find valuable. Often the best salespeople become even better when they realize they were wasting time and energy on something that a client didn't value. If you are doing something for your clients that they don't value, then you *are* wasting your time.

Think back to the fishing analogy from the last chapter. So many salespeople are throwing their lines out to catch one fish at a time. Instead of having one fishing line in the water, a well-funded Trust Bank functions like a fishing net. Every satisfied client with a high balance in their Trust Bank is another line in your fishing net. As you build dozens of highly satisfied clients, you are weaving and stretching your Trust Net across the waters. Soon, you are catching fish that you never even cast a line for.

Find ways to make deposits into your clients' Trust Banks, and avoid making withdrawals. The benefits are irrefutable.

Chapter 3

Your Hippocratic Oath

Why do we trust doctors so quickly?

Think about the first visit to a new doctor. We go into the office of a complete stranger. We often share some of the most intimate secrets about our personal health, behaviors and/or lifestyle within minutes of meeting this person. We remove clothing and allow them to poke and prod us with tools or their hands. They spend a few minutes with us, review the information from the nurse, and they make a decision about what procedures, surgery, and/or medication might get us healthier. Then, we quickly accept these recommendations with the expectation that they *will* help us.

How do we *know* this doctor is trying to help us? Why *don't* we question them the way we question a salesperson? What is their *real* motive? Are they pushing some kind of prescription here? Do they just want to make money and see as many patients as possible? Has the pharmaceutical rep just finished wooing them over a bottle of wine and a round of golf?

I'm not writing these questions to encourage you to doubt your doctor; I just want to make a point of how quickly we trust some people versus how slowly we trust others.

Maybe it is the need for what the doctor can provide that leads us to trust them so quickly. Sometimes we *need* their help or we may actually die. Or, perhaps it is the fact that so many people have gone to that clinic or that doctor and have said good things about them. Or, maybe a gag clause prohibits some people who are wronged from speaking out about their medical malpractice settlements. Or, maybe all the doctors really *are* helping their patients and they have thereby earned this *rapid trust benefit*. Regardless of the reason why we trust them, it cannot be denied that doctors are some of the most quickly trusted people on the planet.

In an effort to further that *rapid trust benefit* doctors recognized long ago the power of a group promise. The Hippocratic Oath was created and adopted as a way of encouraging patients to trust their doctors more quickly. It is a pledge of commitment whereby doctors promise to put their patients' interests above their own. Furthermore, the doctors promise to avoid circumstances whereby their judgment may be compromised when assisting a patient. This helps keep them unbiased in their advice so that they can keep doing what is in the best interest of their patients.

As patients of doctors, The Hippocratic Oath is there to provide comfort to all of us. By pledging to put our interests above theirs, doctors have promised to always do what is best for us first. By following through on that promise over the past several centuries, doctors have earned this *rapid trust benefit* that so significantly increases their efficiency and effectiveness.

This *rapid trust benefit* has always been critical in the medical profession. With a short supply of doctors and a huge demand for their services, doctors have needed to be very efficient with how they use their time. If patients were slower to trust them, then the doctors would waste too much valuable time building trust with new patients instead of healing the sick. The Hippocratic Oath was designed specifically as a way to help us trust our doctors faster so that they could treat more people.

According to U.S. law, right now there is no formal obligation for medical doctors in the United States to officially take and uphold any version of the Hippocratic Oath. However, it is reported that 98 percent of medical doctors in the United States admit to having taken some version of the Hippocratic Oath upon graduation.

Whether Hippocrates actually wrote the Hippocratic Oath, or whether you prefer the verbiage of whatever version of the Hippocratic Oath that your doctor did or did not say when they graduated isn't the point of this chapter. This chapter is about the *spirit* behind the creation and purpose of the Hippocratic Oath.

I believe that most of us are good-meaning, well-intentioned members of society who truly want to help others. I believe that the most successful salespeople have realized that their success is built on doing the right thing for their customers. It is my wish that all salespeople could pledge to follow at least the Golden Rule when acting in their professions: "Do unto others as you would have done unto you."

If we could all pledge to at least treat people the way that we would like to be treated, then we would have a chance at starting to shift the image of what it means to be a person with a career in sales.

Homework Assignment #1:

When you are not at your job, and you have a clear mind, sit down for five minutes with a sheet of paper and a pencil. Set a timer. It doesn't need to take more than five minutes (although it can if you want.) Write down the way *you* would like to be treated if you were *your* customer. When you are done, ask yourself the following questions:

- How many of the ways that you want to be treated are related to politeness, manners, empathy, and listening?
- How many of the things about how you want to be treated are related to the product or service that you are buying?

- How good of a job are you doing at being the best salesperson for a customer like you?
- How many of your customers are like you?
- How would customers who aren't like you want to be treated?

Going through the above exercise and reflecting on your answers to the questions afterward should have a significant impact on your success as a salesperson. Too often we get caught up in our own lives and forget that when we are selling, we are doing a job. If we want to be good at being a salesperson, then we must first commit, *at a minimum*, to following the Golden Rule.

"Treat Others the Way that You Would Like to be Treated."

This is the first commitment of our Hippocratic Oath.

Chapter 4

ALWAYS Do *WHAT* You Say You're Going to Do *WHEN* You Say You're Going to Do It

We already agreed that trust is a critical prerequisite for completing any sale. Whether it is trust in a product, a brand, or your services, it is essential before any sale will be completed. Therefore, it helps to examine how we build trust.

I contend that the primary way that we build trust is simply by following through on our promises. All trust is built on keeping one promise after another, and with each promise kept you make a deposit in your client's Trust Bank. And, for every time that you fail to follow through on a promise, you take a withdrawal. One important note to keep in mind here: *Every* withdrawal is much more significant than *any* deposit. From my experience, you must follow through on at least 20 promises to equal the cost of not following through on one.

For example, you enter a restaurant and are greeted by a friendly person named Tammy who takes your name and puts you on a waitlist (deposit). She then seats you promptly at a nice table (deposit), and your server comes by in a reasonable amount of time (deposit). The server introduces himself as Jeff and asks if you would like a beverage (deposit). You respond with a rather basic order for a beverage of your choice, and Jeff runs away to get it (deposit). Jeff brings you your drink, and it looks like he got it correct (big deposit).

You then proceed to drink your beverage and come away from your cup with a hair in your mouth (*WITHDRAWAL*). All of the nice deposits that were made since you walked into this restaurant were likely completely negated as soon as you realized that the hair in your mouth from your drink was not your own hair. I wish this example were truly fictional, but I can honestly say that this has happened to me personally more than once. The point: Don't make *any* withdrawals from the Trust Bank if you can help it. (By the way, 20 is a totally arbitrary number, and it is completely dependent on the severity of the withdrawal and the significance of the deposits. But 20 seemed like a nice round number, so let's not get hung up on these details.)

While this may seem obvious to so many of you, I have unfortunately found that basic quality service has become a vanishing value in the United States. I grew up in the restaurant business, and I remember going to many restaurants 20 years ago. When my server said that they would do something, they almost always followed through. Doing what you promised to do was simply a way of being. If a server forgot something, then they knew they would get a significant reduction in their tip.

At too many restaurants now, it seems like you are lucky to get what you ordered let alone get it in a reasonable timeframe and the way that you ordered it. Our country's service standards have dropped so low that when the right food comes out just the way we ordered it and on time, we are actually so pleasantly surprised that most of us feel thrilled to give a huge tip. This used to be a normal *minimum!* An increase in tip was usually awarded to a server for having an amazing attitude, providing information, or giving you special assistance that went above and beyond. Now, we are actually just happy to not find hair in our food.

While this absence of follow-through is a huge disappointment for our country, it is a *GIANT OPPORTUNITY* for you! The proverbial "bar" has been set so low, that all we simply need to do to provide *amazing* service is to *do what we say we will do when we say we will do it*. It is really that simple.

Now, for those of you who have already figured this out, I say hooray! But, please keep in mind, many of the people who need to learn from you haven't been taught this simple rule. For whatever reason, some of us learned this concept in our childhood, and others didn't. When you are hiring a new employee, don't just assume that they already understand this. Either weed them out during your interview process, or take two minutes to teach them. Even if you don't hire them, you are doing the world a favor.

Now, just because you *understand* this rule, doesn't necessarily mean that you are great at *following* it. (For example, we all know we are supposed to exercise, eat healthy, get great sleep every night, and drink a minimum amount of water each day. These are pretty basic concepts, but I have yet to meet *anyone* who feels that they are doing all four of these at the right level *every* day.) Following this rule can be challenging. It requires discipline and awareness. It requires you to be *very* careful with your words. It requires you to think before you make *any* promise. Most importantly, however, it requires integrity.

Integrity is built from the commitment that you make to yourself to follow this rule and the self-discipline that you use to keep your commitment.

ALWAYS do WHAT you say you are going to do WHEN you say you are going to do it.

Why do people find this promise so hard to keep? Any time someone doesn't keep their promise, the first thing out of their lips always seems to be some kind of excuse that usually stems from the salesperson's lack of control. (For example: - The cook burnt the food. - The hostess filled your drink, it must be her hair. - Sorry your food is cold; I had to take that order over there and they wouldn't stop talking. - Sorry it's late; I just ran out of time. - Sorry that I said I would be right back and you had to wait on hold for 10 minutes, I had to…)

Any excuse that comes from this vein of thinking is coming from a victim mentality. The service provider or salesperson is saying "Look at me. I'm a victim just like you. Can you believe that this stuff happens to us in this world? I can't control *everything*; therefore, it is okay that I didn't do what I said I would do on time." Let me make this *very* clear:

Customers *DO NOT WANT TO HEAR YOUR EXCUSES.*

Excuses simply mean that you are trying to avoid the blame of not keeping your promise. The excuse is not going to turn the withdrawal from the Trust Bank into a deposit. Most of the time, it doesn't even reduce the size of the withdrawal. It can actually *increase* the size of the withdrawal and further *decrease* the level of trust that your customer has in you.

When you make an excuse that stems from a lack of control of the situation, you are telling the customer that you cannot guarantee the delivery of a quality product or service. You are actually telling them, "Don't trust me, because I might not be able to follow through on my promises."

Once you have failed to follow through on a promise, the damage has already been done. A withdrawal has now been taken from the Trust Bank. Minimizing the impact of the withdrawal is simple: *accept responsibility, make it right,* and *figure out how you can never make this same mistake again.*

Unfortunately, along with a lack of follow through in the service world we have also experienced a severe lack of accountability. Too often I have found my server making excuses as to why food was late/burnt/wrong, and how it wasn't their fault. Or, worse, I've noticed the server try to knowingly slip the mistake by hoping that I wouldn't notice. I always appreciate a server who accepts responsibility for any mistake, makes it right, and hopefully figures out how to avoid this mistake for other customers in the future.

If you ever find yourself unable to follow the rule, because some things are out of your control, then you have two choices: Get them under your control, or don't make that promise.

Some things *should* be under your control. If you are a business owner, then you *should* have minimum standards. If your employees aren't meeting those minimums, then you need to figure out a way to get those minimums met. This is best accomplished by hiring the right people, training them correctly, compensating them fairly, and holding them accountable. Too often business owners decide to just do it all themselves. Whether you are providing a service that is completely dependent on yourself or you are managing a team, you *need* to figure out what things you *can* control.

Then, you need to be sure that your promises, and the promises of your employees, are only made about these things.

A common way that this rule is broken is by *overpromising*. Overpromising is simply saying that you will do something that you can't do or promising to do something sooner than you can get it done. People who make commitments that they never keep on time (if at all) are never fully trusted. With certainty, this is a way to take frequent withdrawals from your client's Trust Bank. One day you may be shocked when you find your client's Trust Bank is empty.

I have seen many salespeople be successful *in spite* of this tendency to overpromise. I have met many people who promise the moon, and their customers have come to expect to get something less and/or later than they were promised; yet, for some reason, the customers keep coming back to this person. It's possible that the product or service is *so* good that they keep coming back because they have no choice. (The demand may be higher than the supply.) Or, maybe they like you as a person, and they want to see *you*. (Your unique way of doing things may add enough value to compensate for your lack of reliability.) Maybe they just don't want to hassle with change. (The pain of switching isn't greater than the convenience of staying the same.) In any case, I assure you that your overpromising *is* hurting your business's potential.

By *under promising* and *overperforming* you will increase your clients' trust levels, and you will be more successful in your business.

ALWAYS do WHAT you say you are going to do WHEN you say you are going to do it.

As simple as this little mantra may seem, it is not so easy to follow through with. But, of all the advice in this book, being impeccable with your word and following through on this promise will have the largest, most significant impact on your business over the years ahead. If you choose one thing from this book to implement and/or attempt to maintain for yourself, please be sure that you will at least try this one.

Over the past 26 years I have built my reputation as a financial advisor on this one commitment. Over my lifetime I have built my reputation on this commitment as well.

Integrity is *everything* in sales. No matter how far back you look in history, the value of someone's word has been paramount. Any effective leader was believed and followed because they did what they said they would do. Keep your promises.

Chapter 5

Know Your Product or Service

As a professional salesperson you are looked at as the expert on your particular product or service. If you don't understand the benefits, uses, limitations, costs, and all other complete ins and outs of your product, then you run the constant risk of making withdrawals from your client's Trust Bank.

Whether you provide food to a customer at a table, or provide insurance to protect your customer from a tragedy, or provide a luxury vehicle, vacation, or other experience, you must *know* your product. Inaccurate information or your inability to provide accurate information will make it impossible to make deposits into your client's Trust Bank.

Worse, it runs the risk of taking withdrawals.

Every time you are able to find out what a client wants to know about your product or service, and you are able to provide a satisfactory answer to your client, you are making a deposit. The deposit is larger if you are able to provide the information *quickly,* and add a little bit of bonus information that the client wanted to know. (The deposit is even larger if the client didn't realize that they wanted to know it until you told them.) If you provide wrong information, however, you will take a huge withdrawal from the Trust Bank as soon as the client discovers the inaccuracy.

When it comes to understanding your product, it is critical to note that the customer *is always right, even when they are wrong.* If a client thinks that you are wrong about your product, it doesn't matter whether the client is correct that you are wrong, or they just *believe* that you are wrong. The withdrawal from their Trust Bank still occurs, and you have just decreased your likelihood of making this prospect a client.

Think of how many times a client or customer has had the wrong idea or knowledge about your product or service.

What do you do? Do you explain that they're wrong? Do you get defensive? Have you ever ended up in what seems to be an argument with your customer about the accuracy of some piece of information? Do you think this helped or hurt you in getting the sale completed?

Let's make this personal. How many times have you, yourself, thought one thing about a product or service only to later discover that you didn't understand it as well as you thought? How did you feel when you found out you were wrong?

Now, if a salesperson had pointed out your ignorance with arrogance, rudeness, or even a little chuckle, how would you have felt? You probably wouldn't want to do business with that person. On the other hand, what if your salesperson caringly shared the correct information with you in a way that didn't make you feel judged or stupid? What if they tactfully educated you on the correct information, and you felt smarter when they were done?

If your client *believes* something that is incorrect about your product or service, then this is a *fact* to your client. If this misbelief will likely result in their later disappointment with your product or service *or* it will prevent your client from choosing your product or service, then it is up to you to correct this misinformation. This is why it is so critical to constantly check in with your client to make sure that they *understand* and *agree* with what you are saying. **As soon as they don't understand**

something, they will stop listening. As soon as they don't agree with something you have said, they will stop trusting you. The better you are at identifying these moments quickly and addressing these issues with your customer, the more successful you will be in sales.

When you discover that your client has misinformation or a misunderstanding, this is a *huge* opportunity for you to either make a big deposit in their Trust Bank or take a big withdrawal. Caring about your client's feelings and being tactful in this moment will make a significant difference.

Chapter 6

No One Cares What You Know Until They Know That You Care

When a customer walks into your office or store, they usually already know that they want to buy something that you offer. With the flow of information available today, they have most likely already researched at least a little bit about your service or your product, and they have determined that they want to buy. **It is not your job to convince someone that they want to buy; it is your job to help the customer buy what they already know they want.**

So many sales are lost because a salesperson is so excited about their product or service that they jump into explaining, demonstrating, and selling it as soon as a potential customer walks in the door. Like an actor waiting for an audience, this type of salesperson is eager to show the customer the product and jump into their pitch so that they can get the sale (and/or get the attention that the salesperson is really craving in life). This may be successful some of the time, and the more passionate that you truly are about your product, the more often this method of selling will be successful. *But*, if you simply add two to five minutes to the beginning of this presentation, then you can significantly increase your frequency of successful sales.

You see, if you jump into a pitch about a product or service as soon as you meet a customer or potential client, they are not really listening. Instead of feeling your passion for the product or service, and instead of learning the exciting information that you are sharing, they are constantly looking at you sideways and wondering over and over in their head: Can I trust this person? Is what they are saying true?

In this situation, the *better* your product or service sounds, the *less* likely you are to sell it. And, there you are, trying to make your product or service sound like it is the greatest invention since sliced bread (or the Internet, or the wheel, etc.) Your prospect is suffering from "sounds too good to be true syndrome." They are doubting the accuracy of your information. Your integrity is under fire. At best, this approach will result with you having to answer a myriad of technical questions that they have come up with during your explanation as they compare your words to their prior knowledge or the research that they have already done on your product. At worst, the prospective client/customer has already mentally shut down somewhere in your presentation. They have decided that they cannot trust your information. You have overwhelmed them and they need to do more research, or they have judged that they don't like you enough or trust you enough to do business with you. Now, they are simply looking for a tactful way that they can leave without completely hurting your feelings. (And, some customers don't really even care if they *do* hurt your feelings.)

So, what do you do here? How can you explain your product or service with the passion that you truly feel without decreasing your likelihood of making this person a client?

Answer: Remember the title of this chapter – No One Cares What You Know Until They Know That You Care.

As I mentioned in my *Note to the Reader,* no one should be reading this book unless they truly care about their clients. For the rest of this book, I will not be using the word *customer.* If you think that you're selling to a *customer* then you are focused on selling your product or service; you are not thinking first about what your product or service will do for your *client*. **A *customer* is someone you sell to. A *client* is someone who you have a relationship with.** If you really care about the person on the other side of that sales table, then you are *always* working with a *client*.

In order for your client to know that you care about them, you need to take some time at the beginning of the conversation to get to know them. Ask them what they are looking for. Ask them why they chose your company to walk into. (Don't be afraid of the answer to this one, by the way. If you are afraid of the answer to that question, then you don't feel very good about where you work. You need to learn why your company *is* great, or you need to find a company that better suits your passion.) Ask them why they are interested in your product or service. These are basics: What do you want? Why do you want it? And, why are you here? The answers to these questions are critical so that you can help the client acquire whatever they already came into your establishment to buy.

Keep in mind, however, that the client *knows* that these answers will empower you. They *know* that these answers will make it easier for you to sell them something. If you ask these questions because you are truly interested in the client, then they are likely to share this information with you. If you ask these questions brusquely, rudely, haphazardly, or disingenuously, then you are telling your client that you don't really care about them. A poorly worded question with a lack of attention at the beginning of a relationship is a sure way to make a huge withdrawal from the Trust Bank. The client will determine that you are either disinterested in helping them or, worse, you are being fake. Being fake, to the client, means that you are trying to get what you want by manipulating them. No one wants to be manipulated, and if a client feels manipulated, they will not want to share the answers to these basic questions.

Think for a moment of how many times that you have been approached by salespeople and used this excuse to stave them off: "I just want to look around." Why didn't you want to talk to those salespeople? Most likely, you didn't want to talk to them because you were still gathering information, and you didn't trust them. Either you believed that they were not trustworthy by their very nature (or the nature of their job) or you didn't trust your own knowledge yet to discern the accuracy of the information that the salesperson might tell you. You did know, however, that you didn't want to be manipulated.

Your clients are feeling the same things. If you *truly* care about your clients, then they *can feel* that when you start talking with them. Don't just ask the three questions that we mentioned above. Ask them about what you really want to know more about. Take a genuine interest in your client. Do they have children? Did they have a good weekend? Do they have travel plans for their summer? Did they have a good holiday? Are they glad the week is almost over? These are all stereotypical questions that good salespeople ask as icebreakers, but the best salespeople really *are* interested in the answer. Find out *specific* things that are *unique* about your clients. This is the beginning of your relationship; learn whatever you can about them. Show them that you care.

If you spend just a few minutes taking a genuine interest in your client *before* you start explaining the product or service that you are passionate about, they are *much* more likely to hear what you are saying. And, if you relate the product or service to the specific needs and desires of that client (that you just learned), then they are much more likely to become your client. They are not just there to buy your product or service; they are there to solve a problem. You want to help them be happy; show them how your product or service will help them increase *their* happiness.

NO ONE cares WHAT YOU KNOW until
they KNOW that YOU CARE.

In almost any profession, by the time you have the opportunity to talk with an interested prospect, they have already concluded that they want your service or product. In many cases, a client has determined that they want your product or service, and they're actually going through the sales process as a way to determine whether *you* are the one qualified to deliver it.

This changes everything about the sales process. It is really an interview, and *you* (the salesperson) are the interviewee. Will you pass? How?

In any sales situation, a customer is always questioning the motives of the salesperson. Unfortunately, this is the condition of the reputation of a salesperson in today's society. (I hope we can one day change this, but for now we must cope with the world we live in.) The first way to gain the trust of your client and pass the interview is to show them that *you are human* and that *you care about them*.

As I mentioned at the beginning of this book, there are, unfortunately, some people in the sales profession who do not care about their clients. They make this much harder for the vast majority of salespeople who *do* care. How will a client know that you are different from the salespeople who only care about themselves? You have to *show* your clients that you care about them.

The easiest way to show your clients that you care is to *listen* to them. When a person feels heard *and* understood, they *automatically* trust you more. It is extremely easy to show that you are listening. Ask questions, and listen for the answer. If it's a complicated answer, then explain it back to the client in your own words. Many times this is all that is necessary to show your client that they have been understood. Then, solve the problem.

PART 2

MORAL HAZARDS AND KEEPING TO THE STRAIGHT AND NARROW

Chapter 7

Law vs. Ethics

Before we examine the typical moral pitfalls that face a salesperson throughout their career, it is important to note that there is a significant difference between what is **legal** and what is **ethical**.

Following the law means, literally, not doing anything that is *illegal*. Being ethical means, literally, not doing anything that is *immoral*. Originally, law was created to hold people accountable and punish those who chose to break society's moral codes. The laws were closely tied to what society believed was morally right and wrong. When someone broke a law, they most often *knew* that they were breaking that law, and society needed a way to make them "fall back in line." If the punished were not able to reform, then they were removed from society through incarceration or capital punishment.

Hundreds of years ago the mass prevalence of religion and spiritual beliefs encouraged people to listen to their inner voice and follow their moral compass. Everyone was told regularly by their parents, church, friends, community, and society exactly what was *right* and what was *wrong*, and most importantly they were told to listen to their hearts. When laws were broken, the sane lawbreakers *knew* that they were willfully breaking the laws.

Over the last several decades human beings have grown more agnostic and unbelieving in their nature. With the advances of science, a wave of skepticism has washed over most of the developed world. Every belief set has been met with a *prove-it* mentality, and, in the absence of proof, people have chosen not to believe. I fear that this approach has led to a situation where we have "thrown the baby out with the bath water."

Please understand that I'm not advocating for any one religion or spiritual belief set here. In fact, I think that most religions and spiritual beliefs are created with a good moral foundation and good intentions. However, as many people in the United States and other developed countries around the world have chosen to remain agnostic, many of them have also chosen to ignore their moral compass. This moral compass is a critical component of who we are as human beings, and it *is* the proverbial "baby" that has been thrown out with the religious "bath water." In the absence of a religious or spiritual upbringing, many members of society have mistakenly sought guidance from the law on what is right and wrong. Too many people are creating their moral compass instead from what is legal and illegal.

Law was not designed to be a good replacement for your moral compass. It was designed instead to prosecute those who already knew they were breaking the rules. With the increasing blindness to our inner voices, we have turned to words like "it's not illegal" to justify our actions that we know in our hearts are not *right*. Then, we use these legal loopholes to break the rules of our moral compass so we can "get ahead" in the moment until laws are written to close those loopholes.

Now we have a legal code that is longer than any lawbook ever written. As each loophole gets closed more laws need to be written. As more laws are written, more people seek legal means of getting around them. It is no wonder that we have such a litigious society. As more and more people are morally wronged, they have to use our legal system to get what they want. Still others, unfortunately, use the imperfect laws and the courts as a means to get *their* way. These laws that were created to actually *protect* the innocent and *convict* the guilty, instead get misapplied by the guilty to punish the innocent.

This book is not written to be a dissertation on the challenges of our legal society or the general increase in agnosticism, but it is imperative as we move forward in our careers as professional salespeople that we do more than just follow the law.

When you are in a position of trust, it is critical that you follow more than just the laws; you must listen to your inner conscience. Whenever you find yourself rationalizing something, your inner conscience is probably telling you that this behavior is ethically wrong. Listen to that voice first.

Follow its guidance. You will be much happier and more successful in the long run.

Chapter 8

The First Moral Pitfall –
Misrepresentation

The first moral pitfall that you will encounter in a career as a professional salesperson will likely be to misrepresent yourself, your company, or your product. Most good companies will counsel you that this is unacceptable behavior and that you will be terminated if you do this. However, there are others that actually teach this behavior and encourage it. Hopefully, you will sense this and listen to your moral compass.

When you get started in a career in sales and you want to convince a client that you are worth listening to, you sometimes feel that you are not worthy of being listened to. Feeling somehow inadequate, you might bolster up your credentials as a way to appear more knowledgeable and increase your probability of closing a sale.

For example, some firms have hundreds of "vice-presidents." In fact, a new sales associate with some firms is immediately given a title like vice-president just so clients will think that the new associate is more experienced.

Does this actually increase sales? Maybe. Some clients might fall for the vice-president title and more quickly agree to purchase something. But, the hit on your long-term credibility is huge. Furthermore, you don't *feel* like a vice-president, and many clients can pick up on that emotion. This strategy can actually backfire if the client believes you. After all, if the inexperienced *you* became vice-president, then what would that say about the quality of the whole company? Or, if they are really savvy, then they see the ploy for what it is and start distrusting you even further.

The response is the same whenever you misrepresent yourself, your company, or your product. Any lie about your experience or credentials, company ranking, company experience or credentials, or product quality or capabilities is a misrepresentation. Even an exaggeration is a misrepresentation.

For example, statements like the following are exaggerations:

- This product is so great, you will never have to replace it. (Everything has a shelf life.)
- I am working with lots of people from … (This is fine if you actually *are* working with lots of people from …, but if you are simply *trying* to work with lots of people from … and are "faking it till you make it", then this is an exaggeration.)
- This is the *best* … (Only say this if you truly *believe* that it is the best.)
- This (company/product) was ranked number one in … (Again, only say this if it's true.)

In fact, the word *exaggeration* is a synonym for *lie*. Don't fool yourself; when you exaggerate the truth you are really just rationalizing a way to feel better about lying.

The thing to remember here is simple: Don't lie. In fact, don't even come close to lying. Your clients can *feel* if you are being dishonest. You may think that you need to be dishonest in the beginning, but you must truly avoid this temptation. It is so much more important to be completely honest with your word.

Just because you are being honest, doesn't mean that you can't point out the good qualities about you, your product, or your company. Look for the good things that you know to be true. Share those good things with your client. As soon as you slip down that slope of bending the truth, you are heading into a moral quagmire. Your clients won't trust you, your reputation will be spoiled, and you won't feel good about the things that you do accomplish.

This policy extends both to communicating an untruth *and* allowing a client to believe an untruth that you recognize. For example, just because *you* didn't lie, doesn't make it okay to ignore a misunderstanding that you have observed your client to have.

Let's imagine the following scenario. A client walks into your store or office and has heard from someone that the best product is X. After they tell you how amazing they think X is, you realize that they are talking about product Y. But, maybe product X pays you more of a commission. You are tempted to sell this client product X, because they have already determined that that is what they want. Do you sell them X or do you tell them about and steer them toward Y?

If your inner conscience isn't firing right now, then you might need to wake it up a bit. Your moral compass should make it abundantly clear that you need to tell them about product Y. If you were (or still are) rationalizing ways to sell them product X because "it's not your fault that they didn't understand" or "purchasing a product is the responsibility of the consumer" or "that's why 'buyer beware' laws are written", then you are going down the wrong path.

Again, the bottom line here: *Be honest.* And, help your client to understand the truth.

As moral pitfalls are significantly easier to avoid when you look at them in advance (without the distraction of temptation), I am hopeful that this book is catching you at a moment in your life when you are truly in touch with your integrity. In the spirit of maintaining your integrity regarding misrepresentation I want to identify and clarify the three different kinds of misrepresentation for you: *intentional misrepresentation, misrepresentation by omission,* and *accidental misrepresentation.*

Intentional misrepresentation is pretty straightforward. It is the first and most obvious kind of misrepresentation, and it is highlighted above. Simply put, this is intentionally communicating something you know and/or believe to be untrue or exaggerated.

Misrepresentation by omission is also pretty clearly understood. The example above of a client misunderstanding a product and a salesperson failing to clarify (or omitting information) is a clear no-no. Remember, this isn't about whether you are going to get away with it because its *legal*; this is about what is *ethical*. Tell the *whole* truth—always.

Accidental misrepresentation is sometimes harder to see, but it is just as big of an issue. Salespeople make mistakes. Sometime in the future, you will be confronted with these facts: 1) You will think something is accurate about the product or service that you are selling. 2) You will discover that what you thought was wrong. 3) You will realize that this misunderstanding of yours led you to previously misrepresent your product or service by accident. – How you handle yourself in this situation will be a true testimony to your integrity and your character. The answer to the question of "What do I do now?" is simple: *LET YOUR CLIENTS KNOW!* Don't just tell your new prospective clients the correct information and think that you are okay. Your previous clients already purchased this product or service from you. They *trusted* you. If they still don't know something that you have now discovered about the product or service they purchased, then you have a moral duty to let them know about it. There are all kinds of tactful ways to handle these situations and save face. Furthermore, if the accidental misrepresentation resulted in a significant difference in the quality of the product or service that your current client is experiencing, then you *need* to find another way to make it up to them.

There are countless examples of big businesses trying to cut corners when they discover that there are defects in their products. Think of every recall that you have ever dealt with. These are moments when companies are *making things right*, and they deserve positive recognition for showing the world to do things the right way.

I have seen countless movies where the plot is about some huge corporate conspiracy. Often that conspiracy is centered on a company deciding that the price of dealing with clients who experience a problem with a product and complain about it is cheaper than the price of issuing a recall and repair of the product. This moral dilemma has been used in these cinematic stories because it creates a true emotional response in the audience. We all *know* the right thing to do. We are all appalled when the company chooses financial reasons over people's lives or safety. Why would you ever put yourself in the same camp as those evil, money-focused, uncaring big businesses that are portrayed so negatively in these movies?

The bottom line on misrepresentation: Don't do it—ever, and, if it happens by accident, then make it right.

Chapter 9

The Second Moral Pitfall – Falling Prey to a Conflict of Interest

Now that you have the trust of your client, you might be tempted to sell them something that they don't need or that they don't want. In fact, you may have a product that you know is better for them, but you will be enticed to sell them something else because of some conflict of interest. Perhaps selling the other product will pay you more. Perhaps you just got a gift or had a nice dinner with the wholesaling representative who works for the inferior product line. You may come up with all kinds of rationalizations, but the bottom line is: Do you believe that this is the best thing for your client?

Objectivity is a true virtue when you are a sales professional. People will trust you with significant amounts of their money that they have worked very hard for. They are exchanging those hard-earned dollars for your product or service. Part of what they are paying for goes to pay for your income.

Whether you are earning that money as a commission or as a salary, it is generated from the proceeds of this sale. Your primary job and what you are being paid for is to help your client **choose the right product for them.** They deserve to get your best and fairest opinion; they are paying you for it.

It is hard to maintain objectivity in just about any sales profession. You are constantly bombarded by wholesalers telling you that their product is the best. You are constantly wooed by gifts, trips, and other sales incentives.

It is even possible that your company is owned by a product provider, and they may want you to sell their product over others that you know to be superior.

Sometimes, the knowledge that you have may feel like a curse. Once you know that something else is better for your client, you have a moral obligation to do the right thing by your client *even if it's harder for you or pays you less money.* In fact, sometimes, this knowledge may mean that you no longer have a product available that you even believe in. You just "learned yourself out of a job."

There are plenty of distributors of inferior products in this world. Every salesperson needs to find a way to work within these limitations ethically. When you have learned yourself out of a job, you have two choices: Quit and start selling something that you believe in, or find out where your product *wins.*

Just about any product or service can beat out the competition in certain circumstances. Some products are perfect for clients in specific life stages – baby food and baby diapers. Other products and services are great for specific types of clients – prescription medications are only for people with the applicable illnesses. Finally, other products are simply more desirable at specific times of the year or to a special demographic – sports tickets only work for sports fans, and snow tires are only needed when there is snow.

While these are pretty obvious and basic examples, whatever your product or service is, it usually has a *sweet spot* when compared to the competition. Find your product's sweet spot. Knowing that your product is the absolute best choice for a particular client in a particular situation will have an amazing effect on your success in sales.

First, you will have complete conviction when you are telling your prospective client that it *is* the best thing for them.

Second, by being aware of the specific type of your ideal client and the specific circumstances of your ideal client, you will naturally become more aware of these people. Through a natural organic growth, your familiarity with your ideal client will result in your discovery that you are surrounded by more prospects than you ever realized. Furthermore, your conviction that your product *is* the best thing for them will lead you to fulfill a moral obligation to share your knowledge about your product with them. After all, when you meet someone who your product is perfect for, they are truly hurting themselves if they aren't using your product.

Chapter 10

The Third Moral Pitfall –
Abuse of Trust for Self Gain

Some salespeople and/or clients may think that there is something wrong with earning more money for selling a more expensive product or service. This is not the case. Selling more expensive items usually requires greater competency in the sales professional. Think of houses, luxury cars, yachts, or intangible products like insurance or securities. The more expensive an item is, the more complicated it usually is. This requires a greater amount of training, education, and licensure, and it may also require more time. Also, for very expensive items, the client may be extremely unique and hard to find. Higher compensation is warranted for more expensive items due to this need for greater competency or the need to find the customers who can afford the more expensive product or service.

However, when you provide multiple products or services, the temptation will always be there to sell the wrong product to a client for the wrong reasons. As is mentioned above, once you have a client's trust, some salespeople may be tempted to abuse it. Perhaps there is a quota that needs to be met, a trip that you want to qualify for, or perhaps you just need to pay your bills. These are all challenging circumstances where an otherwise ethical salesperson might be tempted to fall prey to moral pitfall number three.

The most common abuse of a client's trust occurs when a salesperson chooses to sell a trusting client a more expensive product that generates more revenue for them instead of a less expensive product that might be a better fit for their client. This temptation to abuse a client's trust for self-gain will always be there, and it is up to you to maintain your moral strength and integrity.

This challenge can actually grow even greater the longer you stay in a business. After building trust for decades, many successful salespeople have established a wide Trust Net built with the netting from the overflowing Trust Banks of all the clients they have helped over the years. If you aren't there yet, imagine it. Clients are now pouring into your firm. They want to work with you, and they want your product. They just want you to take care of them, and they are eager to sign whatever you put in front of them. This is a wonderful time, but it is in these environments when the temptation to abuse that trust may be the strongest.

Once you have achieved your own personal success you may start to feel justified to work a little less. Perhaps you even allow your product or service quality to suffer. Or, perhaps you have concluded that you can charge more for your product or service due to your experience. These are all legitimate reasons for you to adjust your schedule and your prices. And, if *you* set the prices for your product or service, then *you* have every right to charge a price that you think is fair.

But, lurking on the other side of this slippery slope lies a monster constantly whispering to abuse your client's trust.

That monster is telling you to sell them the products that pay you the most. In a fee-for-service environment, you can more easily combat this creature. You can charge any price that a willing consumer wants to pay. They know what they are paying, and you are clear with them about what you are charging and what you are providing. However, if you sell a product that pays you a commission, you *must* be careful to avoid the temptations of this whispering beast. If you are paid commissions, then you will be paid differently for selling different products, and that will lead to an environment where you may be more easily tempted to violate moral hazard number three.

I am not advocating for a fee-only environment for all products here. I understand the fairness of compensating a salesperson proportionately to the value that they provide their company. This, after all, is the purpose of paying a commission. When an employer hires someone on a salary, they don't know how productive that employee might be.

They don't know how much value that employee might bring to their company.

Imagine this: Two employees are hired at the same time with the same background of experience and education. They are offered the same salary to start. In the first three months, one of those employees has sold twice the products that the other employee has sold. The more successful employee has earned the company twice the revenue that the other employee has earned. Is it fair that both employees are paid the same? Now imagine that they were both working on commissions. The employee who earned the company twice the revenue and sold twice the products received twice the paycheck.

Commissions are a very fair way of rewarding salespeople for the results from their hard work and effort.

The challenge with commission compensation is that many salespeople sell a variety of products, and some of those products often pay different levels of commissions. This creates an inherent conflict of interest as a salesperson may gravitate toward selling the products that pay them the most. The ethical salesperson must learn to work within this environment. When a commissioned salesperson sacrifices their moral compass by focusing on what pays *them* the most instead of focusing on what is best for their clients, they simultaneously slaughter their own integrity.

There are various ways to combat this dilemma. Initially, I found that the best way to fight this was to actively force yourself not to think about how much money you will make during the sales process. Refuse to let your mind wander to any kind of calculation that compares your earnings from selling one product over another while you are helping a particular client. Once you are done helping the client, and you have assisted them with the best product or service that meets their needs, then you can calculate your earnings. We will call this strategy "Building Your Mental Money Wall."

Some of you may find this strategy helpful, but others of you will automatically know which of your products pay you more than others. For many of you, that knowledge will be challenging to ignore while you are in the sales process.

Ultimately, to maintain your integrity in a commission selling environment you *must* learn to separate your own needs and desires from the needs of your client.

This is easy for some and harder for others. It requires a strong moral compass, and it requires you to be passionate about helping your clients more than yourself. Once you develop this (and some people are born with it), it will be the most important skill that you can develop as a successful salesperson. And, it is critical that you maintain and enhance this skill so that you are never tempted to backslide.

If you are fortunate enough to be able to choose from varying commission options when you sell your products, then try your best to structure your choices in the fairest and most level way possible. For example, I am in the securities and insurance business. Many products are simply not available on a fee-only basis. If I choose not to offer them, then I am limiting my clients' options, and I may be excluding the products that will best meet their needs. To keep the potential conflicts of interest to a minimum for my firm, when they are available we always choose the commission options that pay us one percent of the assets under management per year. By earning the same one percent per year to manage our clients' money, we are truly impartial as to which product or strategy they might choose. We have created a level compensation environment so that our advisors will keep the temptation to sell one product over another limited to reasons that only relate to what is best for our clients.

When you hear the insidious whispers telling you to use that product that pays you more; no one will know; you are still helping your client; it's not illegal; you deserve it; think of all you have done for them; it's still better than what they were getting before... Recognize this voice for what it is: an enemy of your integrity. And, if you decide to follow that voice, remember that it only takes *one* of the lines in your Trust Net to be cut for the whole net to unravel. Pretty soon you have hundreds of interested clients swimming through the hole in your net to one of your more ethical competitors.

PART 3

ADVANCED SELLING TECHNIQUES AND USING THEM ETHICALLY

Chapter 11

Seven Critical Sales Skills to Adopt

For those of you who have been waiting for the specific "How To" of selling, this is the chapter for you. Many of these skills may seem extremely basic, but I encourage you to review the bullet points of this chapter. If you are an experienced salesperson and you find even one new bullet point, it will be extremely helpful. If you are new to a sales profession, then this list will be a priceless reminder of what you *must* integrate into your very being. When you do all of these things naturally, you will be amazing in your career.

Listening and Eye Contact

Again, these may seem obvious, but I must place this at the top of the list. As I mentioned in Chapter 4, no one cares what you know until they know that you care. The easiest and most important way to show that you care about your client is to make eye contact so they know you are listening, and then repeat what they have told you back to them so that they know you understood them.

People are walking around this planet with so many ideas, feelings, thoughts, and interests, but there is a terrible shortage of willing, caring friends to listen to them. You cannot build trust with anyone until they know that they are cared about *and* understood. Look people in the eye, and repeat what they ask or say back to them so that *they know* they are understood.

For those of you who are taking this literally, I do want to clarify something. Don't be a parrot when you are repeating things back to your client. I can just see a detail-oriented student following my instructions and repeating what their client says back to them word for word. At best, your client might think you have to repeat things to remember them. At worst, they might think you are mocking them and storm off. Then, angry at your lost opportunity, you express a few profanities at me and tell me how my book sucks and these ideas are useless.

When you repeat back to your client, make sure you confirm what they were saying in your own words. This also shows that you have heard them *and* integrated their ideas into your own understanding of what they wanted to share.

Speak Clearly and Carefully

Again, this may go without saying, but after hearing so many people in sales professions garble their words or put their foot in their mouth, I feel a need to list this here. Your job is to explain, inform, and persuade someone to purchase a product or service from you that will improve their lives. If you don't speak clearly and think about your words, you will lose countless sales opportunities.

One of the primary places that I look for new people to hire in my company is in a restaurant. Being a server is a great prerequisite for becoming an excellent financial advisor later in life. An exemplary server is fast, efficient, friendly, thoughtful, attentive, articulate, and a great listener.

When you are at a restaurant and your server sounds like he or she is talking through a fast food drive up machine, you worry about the quality of your experience. Will this person understand my order? I can't even understand what they are saying. And, when your server isn't sensitive enough to consider the impact of their words on the people at the table or the tables nearby, then they really aren't tactful enough to be a great financial advisor or great in *any* sales profession.

As sales professionals we are often in positions where we have to educate our clients. Many times those clients have significant egos that we don't want to damage. If you can't speak tactfully to your clients and be sensitive to the impact of your words, you will not likely have much success in a sales profession.

Dress to Impress

I have seen many financial advisors and other sales professionals dress down to meet their clients. I have heard the comments: "My clients show up in shorts. I should meet them looking like them." While I do agree that there is some truth to being similar to your clients (see mirroring and matching later), I think these sales professionals are missing a subtlety that makes a big difference.

Most *new* clients aren't looking to work with someone who is just like them. Maybe your existing clients would appreciate seeing you relaxed and dressed more comfortably in the second and/or third meetings. But, if you are selling anything that is significantly complicated or expensive, your clients want you to look like someone who they would trust and respect.

Think about doctors and lawyers. They don't dress to match their clients. Lawyers are working to connect with the judges, the jury, and their clients. Doctors need to dress neatly and conventionally so that you have confidence in the cleanliness of the hospital and the consistency of their services.

Yes, you may encounter that occasional eccentric person who says to you: "I don't trust anyone in a suit." But, you can always tell them that you wear jeans as soon as you get home, and you had to dress up for the client before or after them.

Or, you can let them know that you dressed up just for them to show them that you take them seriously. If you underdress, the people who think that you didn't dress up enough for their tastes will never tell you that you lost some trust and respect points by not dressing nicely enough for your position.

Mirroring and Matching

Connecting with your clients is very important. One of the best ways to show your clients that you are really listening to them is to change your speech to match theirs. I'm not saying copy their accents here, but if your client is speaking slowly, then slow down your information. If your client speaks quickly, then pick up the tempo.

Clients have developed a comfortable pace of speech for themselves over their lifetime. By matching your pace to theirs you are more likely to help them retain the information that you are sharing.

Many sales professionals have used mirroring and matching for years as a means of manipulating their clients to develop a connection. As I said in the beginning, I truly hope that you are not trying to use these powerful skills to manipulate your clients. But, if your purpose is noble, and you are putting your clients' interests before your own, then you will connect better with them by matching their pace of speech.

If you can do it authentically, you can also assist your connection process by mirroring their posture. Crossing your legs when they cross theirs, breathing at a similar pace, and even folding hands and arms when they do can increase your ability to connect with your clients.

Again, if this is done with the intent of manipulation, your clients will sense that, and you will be doing more harm than good. But, if you are genuinely trying to connect with your client, and you are finding it difficult to get through to them, try subtly matching their posture, breathing, and speech speed. You will likely connect much faster with the people you are trying to help.

Limit Your Clients' Choices

From a psychological standpoint, it is much harder to make a choice between three things as opposed to two. For example: which do you dislike more – liver or brussel sprouts? Maybe you like one of those or both of those, but regardless it's usually easier to answer than this one: Which do you like the most – pizza, ice cream, or chips? It has been psychologically and physiologically proven that the human brain exerts less energy and has a much easier time choosing between two choices instead of three or more. Each additional option exponentially increases the necessary mental energy to make a decision. This is causing unnecessary stress on your clients, and it is making the whole decision making process take longer. In a sales profession, you don't have the luxury of wasting time. Any extra time spent with one client means less time with the next client. (By the way, I may have hit on some favorite foods and/or most hated foods for you, and your choice was easier with the example of three instead of the two mentioned above. I assure you that with more examples you will notice that it is harder for you to make a decision between three items vs. two. Also, for those of you who are wondering, the correct answers are liver and pizza.)

I have seen countless sales professionals make the mistake of telling their prospective clients about *every* option that exists instead of simply narrowing the universe of choices down for them. Don't throw up all of the options to your potential client in a way that is most certainly going to result in them saying, "I need to think about it." Instead, limit the choices to the best two that you think would most suit your client's needs. (By the way, if you limit your choices to only one option, then your client will be making this decision: "Am I going to buy this? Yes or No?" Get ready to handle all the reasons why they might not want what you are selling. If you provide two options, then your client will naturally be thinking: "Do I want this one or that one?" Instead of feeling like you are on opposite sides of a bargaining table, you are on the same side with the client trying to figure out which of your two products is a better fit for them. Which process do you think is more likely to result in a working relationship?)

Check In Regularly With Your Clients When You Are Presenting

If you are talking for a long time as you try to explain a complicated nuance or educate your clients on the details of your product or service, you have to check in with them periodically. As soon as your clients develop a question, they can't listen to what you are saying any longer. They are trying desperately to hang on to that question and not forget it as you continue on in your explanation. By checking in with your clients during the sales process you are much more likely to answer their questions quickly and enable them to listen to the rest of the information that you are sharing.

I find that simply asking my clients periodically if what I just said makes sense helps to confirm that they are engaged and understanding me. As you get better at paying attention to your clients, you will start to notice the change in their facial expressions and body language when they either don't understand something that you just said or they don't agree with it. Either of these is a great opportunity for you to stop your presentation (they aren't listening now anyway), and check in with them. Ask them what you can clarify, and/or learn what they are disagreeing with. The confusion that you clear up will engender more trust and show them that you really are paying attention to them. And, if they disagree with you, then the explanation of their feelings will make it easier for you to determine which of your products and/or services will help them the most. Maybe there is a misunderstanding, or maybe you need to find a better fit for them.

As you get really good at reading your client's body language, you may even notice their response is directly related to something you just said. With experience, you may actually appear to read their minds as they respond similarly to other clients at the same points in your presentation. In these moments, you can sometimes connect with them further by addressing their concerns without even asking about them. If you were correct in reading their body language, then you should see your clients nodding their heads as you give your explanation to their private concerns before they even had a chance to share them with you. This can make you look really good to your clients by showing them that you are experienced in working with other people who think just like them, and it shows them that you really understand the way that your clients think and feel. These are both great things to be able to communicate with your client. However, it is still important to check in regularly and be sure that their *complete* question or concern is addressed. If there is a subtle difference between what you thought they were concerned with and what you addressed, then that difference may still stop them from listening further. Additionally, it may even make them feel like you *don't* understand them. The safest way to be sure that you addressed their questions or concerns is simply to ask.

Be Positive, Happy, and Optimistic

In general, people prefer to be around other people who are happy and upbeat. Hopefully, you are naturally a positive, happy, and optimistic person. Many of my clients have indicated that one of the biggest reasons why they work with me is because I make them feel so much better about everything. Some clients have communicated that they come to see me to get their regular dose of optimism.

What is my key to happiness? Fortunately, I have found my own answers to many of the things that cause stress in our lives. Pondering on the various philosophical meanings of life has led me to find answers that provide me with comfort and satisfaction. I *do* believe that amazing things are ahead of us, and I *do* believe in the general goodness of the world. Like all of us, I get confronted with challenges in my life. I experience sadness, anger, frustration, disappointment, grief, and all the other emotions that we generally judge as negative in our society. However, I have learned ways of addressing these that I feel are healthy for me. Furthermore, if I am dealing with a particularly negative experience outside of the office, I find that my emotions about it will still be waiting there for me to reflect on and digest at the end of the work day.

By believing so strongly in the products and services that I provide, and knowing how much I will be helping my clients, I get truly excited, happy and optimistic to change the lives of each client that I get to interact with. If you love what you do, and you are passionate about the people you are doing it for, then you will find it hard to be anything but happy when you are doing it.

Be sure that you love what you do and you love who you are doing it for, and do a little soul-searching to find your own sense of inner peace.

Chapter 12

What *Not* to Do

Some people learn best by being told what *to* do. However, there are certainly lessons to be learned from looking at what *not* to do. This chapter is in some ways an acknowledgement of some of the old-school sales tactics that truly deserve to be buried. To illustrate this, I have written this section as a message to the most experienced sales professionals who are still using some of these methods.

WHY THE OLD-SCHOOL TACTICS DON'T WORK ANYMORE: FREEDOM OF INFORMATION AND GLOBAL CONNECTEDNESS

Some of you salespeople out there may be reading this and thinking: "That young whippersnapper doesn't know what he's talking about. I've been in sales my whole life, and I was taught all kinds of sales techniques and tactics. I use them every day, and I sell more XXXXX than he could ever dream of selling." (Those X's are meant to be your product, by the way, not profanity.)

Maybe you do sell more XXXXX than I do. Maybe your techniques are working. Maybe you have rationalized your techniques over all of these years as justifiable because you believe "that's the only way to sell," "if it ain't broke don't fix it," or because "in the end, I am helping people get what is right for them." Please heed this warning. Many of the old-school methods of selling are, by their very nature, manipulative and misleading. While you may employ some of these methods out of the goodness of your heart and believe that the end justifies the means, these methods will turn off many of your potential clients. Furthermore, they will turn off many of the new salespeople who should be your apprentices in this profession.

If you have been in a sales career for any amount of time, and you still believe that the top salesperson is the person who most takes advantage of the client, then I am urging you to open your eyes wider. Clients are not stupid. If they don't know that you took advantage of them immediately after you sell them something, then they *will* eventually figure it out.

When they do, they will feel conned. They *will not* forget that *you* are the one who conned them. They will tell *everyone* they know how you and your company took advantage of them, and your opportunity for repeat sales and new clients will be destroyed. Thanks to the Internet and our globally connected world, their voices carry further than ever and move like lightning.

To the contrary, if you do a great job helping to assist someone in their pursuit of happiness, then they *will* tell *everyone*. The happier you make someone because of their interaction with you, the more likely they will spread stories of their positive experience to many more people. It is imperative that you remember this when you are faced with those moral dilemmas that confront us every day.

The biggest obstacle to improving our image as noble salespeople comes from selfish moments and shortsighted thinking. If you are managing a team of salespeople, and you are instructing them to cut corners, behave dishonestly or manipulate clients so that you can achieve some internal sales goal, I am begging you to STOP! If you are acting under the belief that you are not going to be around in this job long enough to care about repeat business, I am asking you to STOP thinking that way! It is this shortsighted mindset that leads you to compromise your clients' interests in favor of your own. It is in that moment that you officially become the stereotype that the rest of us fear and loathe. It is that kind of thinking that damages your reputation, your career, and the image of all salespeople across the planet.

Here are five of the most commonly used outdated sales tactics. I hope that you never find yourself using these tactics to get a sale. If you do, forgive yourself, make it right, and never do it again.

The Shut Up and Stare

One of the classic methods of getting a client to commit to a sale is to finish your presentation and be quiet for as long as possible while you wait for the client to sign. The client has somehow run out of objections, and they are forced to sit and think about why they might not want to do what you are saying. Their gut is still telling them that they shouldn't do this right now, but you are sitting there across from them, and they don't want to tell you no. Somehow they feel that if they don't give you a good enough reason, you will make them feel stupid for saying no. Even though their gut says that they don't want to make this decision, they really can't come up with a good reason. In silence, you two sit there and stare at each other. You both know that the first one to speak *loses,* and *you* are determined to *win*.

While this kind of psychological warfare may be successful in closing some sales faster, I do not believe that it leaves your clients feeling like they have made a good decision. Instead of wearing them down, I recommend asking them about why they are hesitating. Ask them if there are any reasons why this isn't a good idea. Then, offer to help them take care of this now. If they need a night to think about things, then let them think about things. But, you must hold them accountable.

Too often clients are saying they need to think about it, but they really aren't going to think about it. They are going to procrastinate on this issue, waste time, and not take care of whatever problem they came to you to fix. Set a deadline and hold them to it. Make them commit to moving forward if they are interested, and be pleasantly persistent about helping them buy your product or service.

In the end, holding them accountable to their commitments, and respecting their process of decision making, will lead to a much stronger relationship and a client who will likely rave about how much you helped them.

Fear Tactics

I can't tell you how often I have seen salespeople use fear to sell something. All you have to do is turn on the television and watch a handful of commercials. Fear is a very powerful emotion, and using fear can motivate people to take action when they normally wouldn't.

While I do believe that there are genuine risks that you may be obligated to communicate to your clients, I do not believe in intentionally using strong, emotionally charged words to implant fear in your clients as a way to sell. Again, while this may work well in many circumstances, it is just plain wrong.

Yes, you can make someone afraid of something. Then, you can provide the cure for their fear. Then they buy your cure and feel better. You are leaving them with a good feeling (you fixed their fear), but instilling fear into another person is emotionally manipulative. It is not my intention to manipulate and control the emotions of my clients. I wish to educate them, inform them, empower them, and motivate them through working together. Part of informing someone and educating someone involves making them aware of any risks that they are exposed to. A significant part of selling is about showing your client a different perspective so that they can more clearly see the benefits of your product or service.

However, showing them a perspective designed to instill fear in them and then producing a remedy to that fear is not acting with integrity.

It is impossible for someone to make a rational choice when they are in an extreme state of fear. By instilling fear in your prospective client, you are intentionally taking them out of a rational state where they might naturally choose your product or service, and you are instead scaring them into it. Later on, when they are no longer afraid, they will see the manipulation that you used, and they will feel that same feeling of being conned. No sale is worth the risk of your client later telling everyone about how you conned them. And, why would you want to spread fear in this world anyway?

Bait and Switch

While this practice is clearly illegal, it is still used in many sales situations to this day. The bait and switch is the idea that you advertise one thing to get your client to come in, but you turn around and switch it to something else when they get there.

I remember a great episode from the show *Growing Pains* that illustrated this point perfectly. Kirk Cameron's character, Mike, was a boy in his late teens who had just started his first job as a salesperson at an audio/video store. His father, Jason, came in to visit him and saw that his son was working with a client. Patiently waiting for his son to finish with the client, Jason observed his son's sales process.

The client came in already knowing what he wanted. He asked Mike for a specific television that he had seen advertised in the paper that morning. Mike leaned forward to the client, looked around to make sure no one else was paying attention, and he quietly explained that the TV from the ad is a horrible purchase. Instead he convinced the client to buy a different TV that Mike assured him was a better deal. Proud to see his son doing so well in his first job and going out of his way to help his client, Jason approached his son to congratulate him.

After complimenting his boy on a job well done, Jason expressed his interest in buying a TV also. Mike quickly told his dad that he should take advantage of the great deal going on right now and buy the television that was advertised in the newspaper.

Confused, Jason looked at his son and said, "I thought you just told that client that this wasn't a very good TV?" Naïvely, Mike explained to his father that this was what they were taught to do. He said that his boss told him how the television in the ad doesn't make the company very much money, and it doesn't pay as much of a commission. The boss told Mike that he was to steer the clients toward a more expensive product that made the company more money and paid Mike more of a commission. But, since this was his dad, Mike wanted to make sure that his dad got the best deal.

Frustrated, disappointed and saddened, Jason looked at his son and admonished him. He explained how what he was doing wasn't right. He further explained that his son's boss had taught him to use an unethical sales practice known as bait and switch. This set the stage for a great learning moment as the son discovered the importance of ethics in selling.

While this story is an excellent example of Bait and Switch and what not to do, it also illustrates one of the key problems in our society right now. Some children just don't know better. Originally Mike was taught that this was a normal way of doing his job. It's possible that Mike's inner voice, his conscience, had fired when his boss told him to sell this way. But, it's also possible that he didn't hear anything from his moral compass. In these moments, the young, impressionable trainees are relying on the education and direction of their mentors. Luckily, Mike had a mentor that he trusted more than his unethical boss – his father. If Mike's father had been out of the picture or Mike trusted the boss more than his father, then he could have been led down a path of unethical behavior. This could have been the beginning of a very long slippery slope into a life of crime.

It is our responsibility as ethical salespeople not to just sell ethically, but to teach others to sell ethically as well. In many ways, this book was written to fulfill this duty for myself by educating more people on the importance of selling ethically. There are more naïve people like Mike out there today than ever before. And, sadly, there are fewer and fewer Jasons out there holding kids accountable and showing them the right way to do things. I hope this book motivates you to be a little more like Jason.

Good Cop/Bad Cop

We have all seen this tactic used by cops in movies. This is a very intentional intimidation tactic that is designed to get a witness to reveal information that they might otherwise not share. It is illustrated in hundreds of movies largely because it is so effective that it has become a regular means of working with suspects to get information.

A person playing bad cop comes into an interrogation room and yells, threatens and intimidates a witness. Then he leaves and another person comes in acting nice and helpful trying to gain the witness's trust. They go back and forth a few times with the good cop often saying that they are on the witness's side, and that they are sorry that the bad cop is so upset.

By making the witness believe that these two cops don't agree with each other, the deceived witness trusts the good cop.

This tactic is often used in selling situations by a team of salespeople to motivate a client to move faster or pay more for a product than they normally would. It can also be used by an individual salesperson who is working with another party to the sale that he "has no control over." It is manipulative and deceitful, and it often results in clients making irrational decisions that are not in their best interests.

There are several strategies that unethical salespeople might use when they are playing good cop/bad cop. One of the most common strategies that we see is this one: A client is making a decision on whether or not they want to buy something. One salesperson takes the other one aside and pretends that they don't want to sell this product to this client at this price while the other one insists that the client gets the "good deal." They do this within earshot of the client so that the client feels like they are getting a better deal than the really are. Believing that they are getting a great deal in this process, the client stops thinking about whether or not they want to buy. Instead, the client quickly (and irrationally) concludes on moving forward with the purchase.

In other situations, a client may ask for something that has to be "checked on" with a manager. The salesperson goes to see the manager while the client waits and sweats it out. In some situations, the salesperson may not even be talking to a manager. Instead, they come back and pretend to have talked to their manager who is unwilling to budge on a particular price or request. Alternatively, the salesperson uses the client's trust to convince them that they played the good cop against the bad cop manager, and they got them the best deal that could be had.

All of these actions are not inherently wrong *if* people are doing what they actually say they will do, *and* they believe in what they are actually saying. Sometimes things really *do* need to be checked on with a manager. Sometimes people really *are* unsure if they can sell a particular product at a particular price to a particular client. However, when any of these salespeople are lying about what they believe or what they are doing, then this behavior has just become an unethical sales tactic.

The lesson here: Be honest, and make sure the others you work with are honest too. Anytime you are part of a deceitful sales process you are acting unethically. Do not try to manipulate your clients' emotions through lies.

It's Going Away

One of the most common ways to short circuit a client's process of decision making is to make them believe that the product you are selling is artificially going away. In an attempt to make someone move faster and make decisions without thinking them through, salespeople might often use this tactic.

Like any of the above examples, this one is very hard on a client. Sometimes discounts and products really *are* going away. When a product is not going to be there much longer, we naturally have urgency inside of us to grab this thing before it is gone.

Creating a false impression of scarcity is another manipulation of clients' emotions to complete a sale. The problem isn't the scarcity itself. Some products and/or deals on products really *are* rare. As an ethical salesperson you have an obligation to tell your client about the rarity of your product or the price of your product. However, pretending that a product or price is rare to motivate a client to *buy now* is completely unethical.

While there are many other examples of what NOT to do, these should give you an idea of the sorts of manipulations that have damaged the image of what it is to be a salesperson. By identifying and clarifying these inappropriate tactics I am hopeful that you will never be tempted to use any of these methods. And, again, if you are using any of these now, please stop.

Chapter 13

Passionate Ambivalence

Now that we have discussed some critical sales habits and several examples of what NOT to do, I can share my best advice on HOW to sell with authenticity and integrity – Passionate Ambivalence. To teach you what I mean when I say "passionate ambivalence" I need to take you to the beginning of a sales career. For those of you who have been selling for awhile, try to remember the early stages of your career. And, for those of you who are just getting started, this should hit home pretty well.

Think about the times when you were in a spot where you *needed* that sale. Do you remember how you felt? Worried? Stressed? Scared? Hungry? Desperate? When you first get started in this business, times come when you really *need* a sale. Bills are tight. You need to eat or keep that roof over your head. Others may be depending on you.

There are pros and cons to these moments. The biggest pro – these situations can show us what we are truly capable of. We can often dig deeper and work harder than we might have ever thought possible. They can help us conquer some internal fears: fear of the phone, fear of prospecting, fear of asking for referrals – fear of rejection. However, how do you think this *neediness* comes off to our prospects...to our clients?

Sometimes you can get lucky. Your neediness can be misinterpreted as passion and actually help you sell, but, more often than not, when a prospect or client senses that *you* need this sale more than they do, all their warning bells go off.

Your odds of successfully closing that sale have withered drastically. Why?

Their alarm bells are going off because of the biggest con to these situations – these needy moments are the moments when a salesperson is most tempted to use unethical sales practices. These are the moments when a salesperson might not want to tell the whole truth. They may want to close this sale faster so that they can get their bills paid. These are the times when their conscience is under fire. As difficult as these times are, this is a critical experience that most sales professionals need to endure and conquer. These situations will test a salesperson's true commitment to ethics.

Now, think about when you've been on a roll. Somehow, you close every sales opportunity that presents itself. Every prospect that you meet, heck, every *person* you meet, becomes a client. You are telling everyone about what you do, how much you love your products or services, and everyone wants to buy. What was different? What keeps us on that roll?

You may believe that it's because you *expect* to win. Like so many gurus tell us, "When we believe it, we will see it." Perhaps that's true. Maybe believing is the key to success.

But, I argue that a true, practical pathway to successfully closing more sales (and thereby helping more people), is to avoid attachment to the outcome of any sale. When you have been successful in every sale that you have had in front of you, all of the neediness that a prospective client might sense is gone. In fact, you don't really *need* that sale. You have tons of other clients that you are already working with. You are personally ambivalent as to whether or not the prospect across from you decides to become a client or not.

While you may have very strong feelings about the benefits of your product or service *for your client,* you have effectively detached yourself from any personal benefits that affect *you.* In this moment, the small amount of personal gain that you obtain from this client's choice to work with you has become so insignificant that it has *no* impact on your sales presentation, your thoughts, or even your feelings. You have completely convinced yourself that this client's decision will not affect your own Happiness.

I call this state of mind: Passionate Ambivalence.

For some of you, this may seem hard to digest. Passionate Ambivalence, after all, is an oxymoron (jumbo shrimp, awfully good, bittersweet, etc.) The word *ambivalence* implies a lack of caring, and yet it is preceded by *passionate* which is truly the deepest form of caring one can have. Please allow me to further clarify my meaning of these words. I do not want you to be ambivalent about your products or services. I do not want you to be ambivalent about your belief that your products or services *are* the best way for your prospect to get what they want or need. These are two things that you *must* be passionate about. But, I *do* want you to be ambivalent about the benefits for you from the outcome of your sale.

To do this, it is helpful first to acknowledge the reality of all sales situations. We must recognize that every prospect is making a *buying decision. They* are making the decision, not *us*. Therefore, the decision is truly out of our control. Ultimately, it is their job to determine their own destiny. Whether or not they buy that product or service and believe that your passion *is* right for them, is ultimately not your choice.

Am I saying that because you can't control the client's decision, you shouldn't practice your communication skills, learn everything you can about your products or services, and learn all you can about the commonalities of your prospects and clients? No. Obviously, that is not what I am saying. Your ability to effectively do your job will *absolutely* have an impact on your overall success. But, never attach the success of your overall business to whether or not you close that individual sale right in front of you. You can't control the buying decision. You don't get the final say. Respect that.

Respect the power of that decision, and respect that your client has to make that decision. If you truly believe in your product or service, then you already know that the choice to buy it will make them happier. But, they still have to make that choice.

For those of you who have been burdened by the duty to help your clients, this is a huge opportunity for you to forgive yourself. When you truly believe that your product or service will be the difference between immeasurably better happiness for your client or increasing sadness, you can start to feel the yoke of responsibility to make those clients do what you *know* they should. Every time someone doesn't do what you insisted you actually punish yourself. Feeling the responsibility for their decision, you bathe in that guilt and question how you could have done your job better.

Asking how you could have done your job better and exploring the answer is healthy, and it will lead to more success. However, feeling responsible for the choices of your client is not. Take a deep breath. Rest easier. You can't control everything. It's not your fault if someone didn't take your advice, and they are now worse off for it. The world works in mysterious ways. Maybe that path that looks so obviously less happy to you was in fact a path they needed to take for all kinds of other reasons that you will never understand. You can't know everything. Maybe they needed to sacrifice some of their happiness just so that you would learn to do your job even better. If you close every sale, you can start to grow complacent. You have to lose some opportunities to learn and to appreciate what you have.

This concept may seem a bit esoteric, so I want to give you a specific example of what I am talking about. One of the products that I work with is life insurance. There are countless ways to use life insurance in wealth management, and there are many amazing ways to capitalize on the tax treatment of life insurance for the benefit of our clients.

However, the first and most important use of life insurance is to provide a sum of money to help survivors after someone has died.

I am passionate about helping my clients to protect this risk. I have seen and heard too many stories about young parents who have died early and left behind children and other loved ones to struggle through life without their parents' financial assistance. There are types of life insurance that are so inexpensive, that there is no legitimate excuse for a parent to not have adequate coverage for their children.

Passionately, I will teach the importance of life insurance to my clients. Carefully, I will explain and educate them on the correct amounts of life insurance and review their options. Professionally, I will give my top two recommendations for them to choose from. Ambivalently, I will allow them to make their decision.

If they choose not to purchase adequate insurance, and then one of them dies shortly afterward, I cannot take on the guilt and responsibility of their choice. Once I have done the *best* job that I can do explaining the risks and the options available, I cannot allow myself to feel guilty if they chose not to protect their families. Once I am done, if I truly did my best, then that was the most that I could do.

When the client senses that you are passionately helping them, *and* you are ambivalent about their decision to protect themselves, *then* they realize that this is their moment to take this decision-making responsibility into their own hands. *They* must make a choice. The client cannot make any excuses about being *sold* or *conned* into purchasing your product. No warning bells are firing that are making them question your motives. If you are truly passionate about helping your clients and you are ambivalent about their final choice, then you will help so many people make the right decisions for themselves. You aren't forcing them or manipulating them down the path that you believe is the best path for them. You are empowering them to choose their own path.

Chapter 14

Respect Yourself and Choose Your Clients

Life is short, and you have a right to be happy. The difference between a customer and a client (as we discussed earlier) is that a customer is someone you sell a product to whereas a client is someone you have a relationship with.

When you have a relationship with someone, you also get to choose whether or not you want to be in that relationship. If a client of yours is disrespectful, rude, negative, or is in any other way undesirable for you, then you have a right to decide not to work with them.

Early on in a sales career, you believe that you need to work with *everyone* who is willing to work with you. The need to sell in order to keep your job or be successful leads you to putting up with just about anyone who will say "yes." After you have been in your career for a while (and the sooner you realize this, the better), you should eventually come to the conclusion that some people just aren't worth the stress and aggravation of maintaining a relationship.

This chapter is about me giving you permission (if you need it) to *fire* your worst clients.

There are lots of reasons not to work with someone. Some are financial – they take too much of your time, they don't generate enough revenue, they are too litigious and might be a compliance risk. Some are emotional – they are rude to you or your team, they have strong contrasting values to yours, or maybe you just don't like them. The more specialized you are at your job and the better that you get at it, the more selective you can be about who you choose to work with.

Servers, for example, may lose their job if they refuse to take care of the clients at a particular table. If, however, you own the restaurant, you have every right to refuse service to someone who is abusing your wait staff and/or disrespecting the rules of your establishment.

Lawyers have the right and the responsibility to carefully choose which cases they are willing to take. Doctors get to choose which patients they are willing to work with. Why wouldn't you use your right to *choose* the people that you have relationships with?

If you are not in a position where you can simply fire your clients (the server above for example), then you do at least have the right to decide if you are going to service your customers as *customers* or as *clients*. Remember, it is the *clients* you will have a relationship with that will expand your business through referrals. The *customers* will get only the basic services that your job has to offer.

Now that you have decided who you like to work with, the next step is for you to specialize even further. A specialist always earns more than a generalist. A heart surgeon makes more money than a general practitioner. A luxury home realtor earns more than a general property realtor. A criminal law defense attorney usually earns more than a generalist attorney with a broad legal practice. The more you specialize in your career the more money you can earn, and the more you can fill your day with the kinds of people you love to work with.

If you already have a job in sales, then think about your favorite product or service that you provide. What kind of person benefits *the most* from that? You want to maintain your integrity and ethics in selling, so it will be much easier for you to be passionate about how much your product or service will help your client if you know who the ideal client is for your product or service. Think about who that person is. How old are they? Are they single or married? Do they have children? What kind of profession do they have? What kind of income do they have? Narrow your target market down in your mind to this specific group of people. Now, ask yourself this question: Do you like people like this?

If you like these kinds of people, then you are in a wonderful situation. Your favorite product will best help your favorite kinds of people. Start to think about what these people have in common. Where do they spend their time? What kinds of things might stop them from buying your product or service? When will they be most interested in learning about and buying your product or service? As you answer these questions you should develop an even better understanding of these kinds of people. This will help you figure out how to get introduced to more people who *are* your ideal clients.

If you determined that you don't particularly like these people who are best suited for the product that you like, then you have some choices to make.

1. You can keep selling to people you don't enjoy being around because you like the product so much. But, you will likely focus on the product's capabilities instead of your client, and you will have to stand out as such an *expert* in your product that these clients have no choice but to find you and work with you.

2. You can try to transition into a job that is not focused on selling to these customers. Perhaps you would be happier managing other salespeople or even wholesaling your product to other salespeople?

3. You can try to learn to like the group of people who are perfect for your product. Perhaps, over time, you can change to enjoy the people that you are working with. Be careful, however, because the less you like and respect your clients, the more susceptible you will be to engage in those aforementioned unethical sales practices.

4. Lastly, you can find another product that you are passionate about.

If you are not already passionate about a product, or you are passionate instead about working with a group of people, then you should focus on the group of people that you like working with. Instead of asking the above questions about who benefits most from your product, start asking these questions: What kinds of things do the people I like working with buy? What products do they buy for work, home, personal fun, etc.? What services do they use, and how often do they use them? Am I passionate about providing any of those services? Could I be passionate about providing them any of those products? What do I need to do to learn about those products so that I can add value and create my career?

As a professional salesperson, you can design the lifestyle that you want to lead. Start either with the product or service that you want to provide *or* start with the types of people that you want to provide those products or services to. But, remember this: *the responsibility to design a lifestyle working with the products or services you are passionate about and working with the people you love is yours.*

Chapter 15

Know Yourself, Know What You Want, and Be Real

This chapter is more of a comment on the philosophy of enjoying life than anything else. However, it may be the most valuable chapter in this book. It's short, so you should just read it; then, you can decide if it was worth your time.

Working in the financial services field I have sat across the table from thousands of retiring Americans. I can tell you without hesitation or reservation that over 70 percent of the Americans that I have helped to retire have been miserable in their careers. Perhaps they started their careers in the beginning with some amount of joy and enthusiasm. Over time, due to undesirable coworkers, changes in the way business is done, or the simple wearing down of their resolve, their hope, and their satisfaction, they grew to be miserable at work.

To the contrary, I have found that about 30 percent of my retiring Americans absolutely *LOVE* their jobs. Some of them celebrate the end of their careers with an enthusiastic look forward to their next adventure in retirement. Others love their careers so much that they never really want to stop working. Instead of *retirement*, we focus more on *financial independence* so that they *can* stop, but *they* will decide when they want to stop.

Too often I have found that the unhappy 70 percent have lost conviction in the belief that they are making a difference. They are truly *punching a clock* and collecting a paycheck.

Everybody in this group really is *working for the weekends*.

My request of you in your careers as you move forward is the same request that I have of all of my employees: Find something you *love* and are *passionate* about. Do something where you *know* you are making a difference. Just as I am ambivalent about my clients choosing to work with me, I am ambivalent about my employees choosing to work in my firm. My goal is to have each of them *love* 80 percent or more of their jobs. We work hard to find people who fit those descriptions. If everyone *loves* what they do, then your work environment *will* be amazing.

The best way that I have found to lead my employees down a path of discovering what they love to do has been to start with these homework assignments. I encourage you to try them out. Do one per day for four days in a row. I assure you that you will find the time was worthwhile.

Homework Assignment #2:

Write down on a sheet of paper (or type into a computer) a list of 100 things that you have already accomplished in your lifetime. These can be things like: finishing first in a swimming race as a teenager, reading a certain number of books, hitting a certain GPA in high school or college, meeting your spouse, visiting a particular country, participating in a charity, having children, etc.

As I have done this, I assure you that the first 20 – 50 come a lot easier than the last 50. Be sure you get *all the way* to 100.

Homework Assignment #3:

Go through your list and circle the top 10 things that mean the most to you. This exercise should teach you something about yourself. It will show you what you really value in your life. Hopefully, this will provide an insight into what you want for your future. Reflect and take it in. Did you learn anything about yourself? Were you surprised by anything? Will it make a difference in what you do with the rest of your life?

Homework Assignment #4:

It's time to make another list of 100 things. List out the things that you want to accomplish before you die. Be sure that you get to a full list of 100 things you want to accomplish. The more time that you took doing Homework Assignments #2 and #3, the easier #4 will be.

Homework Assignment #5:

Go through your list and circle your top 10 most important ones. One of these, if accomplished, will likely help you complete several of the others. Identify that one. This is the most important item on your list for now. Plan to spend at least five to fifteen minutes per day on completing that task. Put it on your calendar. Make it a habit. If it will require a lifetime to fulfill, then adopt the habit for 21 days or more before you decide to add anything else from the list. Once you have completed this item or you have integrated it into your everyday life, then move on to the next item.

(This paragraph is for those of you who are wondering where Homework Assignment #1 was. For those of you who already know, you can skip this paragraph and move on to the next one. Homework Assignment #1 was on page 15 in Chapter 3. I intentionally separated the homework assignments to identify *you*, the person who didn't do your homework. How do I know you didn't do it? You didn't do it, because you would have remembered doing it and not asked *where* Homework Assignment #1 was. I'm guessing, since you didn't do Homework Assignment #1, that you may not have just yet completed Homework Assignments #2 through #5. For your convenience and to encourage you to *do* your homework, I have included five pages following this chapter for you to complete your assignments. *Please* try them. It *will* be worth your time. And, I am only being hard on you because I really *do* care about you.)

These assignments are some of the first exercises that I have every new employee do at my firm. They share their results with me, and then I know exactly what makes them happy. My life is not about making money any longer. I could retire and watch movies, write books, or play video games for the rest of my life if that is what I wanted to do. But none of that gets me excited in the morning. I discovered my life's mission and purpose. My mission: **to empower my clients and associates in their journey to achieve their unique vision of Happiness.** How can I dream of doing that if I don't know what makes each of my employees happy?

I hope that the exercises from this chapter have helped you get to know who you are and what you really value. I hope they have helped you find out what you really want out of life. And, lastly, I hope they have awakened you to make the choice to go after it. Find *your* mission. Nothing happens without taking some form of action. What are you going to do *today* to make your life better tomorrow?

Conclusion

The Rest of Your Hippocratic Oath

In Chapter 3 we discussed the first commitment of your Hippocratic Oath – Do unto others as you would have done unto you. Whether you paraphrase this as treat others as you want to be treated or use the old school language above, the gist of the Golden Rule remains the same. What will the rest of your Hippocratic Oath be?

I was in a room recently with about 30 of this country's most successful business owners. The leader of our group, a man of significant wisdom, posed a question that was extremely enlightening to me. He asked us to define integrity.

As he paused so we could reflect, I thought about my own definition of integrity. After a few moments he shared this insight with us. Regardless of the definition of integrity that we came up with, we were guaranteed to be at least subtly different from everyone else in that room. In that room, at that time, there were 30 different definitions of integrity.

As I reflected on this I realized something significant. *Ethics* is a little different for every one of us. Our moral compasses might fire very similarly, but some of ours might have different volumes and intensities for different circumstances.

In a world like this, how can any consumer learn to trust a salesperson?

We need our own Hippocratic Oath. I don't know how we can make all the potential clients in this world believe us, but we need to create some kind of a commitment to a uniform agreement that puts our clients' needs above our own. This is the only way that salespeople will ever gain the respect and trust that doctors have. This is the only way we can create a doctor's rapid-trust benefit. This is the only way that clients will ever relax so that we can help more people in their pursuit of happiness. I propose that a first draft of this Hippocratic Oath for sales professionals might look something like this:

"As an Honorable Sales Professional, I, (state your name), promise to obey the sales professional code of ethics. In all circumstances where I am working with my clients or prospective clients, I agree to act as a fiduciary. I commit to put my client's interests above all others. I will be honest in all ways about any risks, costs, and disadvantages surrounding my products or services. I promise to disclose and I will seek to minimize or eliminate any potential conflicts of interest. At all times, I vow to share my honest opinion of what I believe is best for my client."

As you can see, this references a "code of ethics" that isn't yet created, but I think we can put together something that would stand the test of time. Perhaps, one day in the near future, we can create the equivalent of an honest salespersons' guild. We can have a group of like-minded sales professionals who agree to abide by this simple code of ethics. Perhaps, over time, we can show the rest of the world that there are *honest* sales professionals who act with *integrity* and *authenticity*.

Appendix

Concepts and terms discussed in this book in order of appearance:

Acknowledgements

There are countless friends, family members, and colleagues who have helped me over the years and thereby made this book possible. From motivational speakers, to coaching programs, to authors and teachers – I could truly write a whole book just on acknowledgments.

First, I want to thank again my wife, Crystal, and my parents, Dennis and Shelley. Without their love, support, insight, and wisdom none of this would have been possible. Second, I want to thank my team at Clear Financial Partners. Without your help, I never would have found the time to get this done. Third, I want to send a special thanks to my friends Bryan Clinard and Jeff Gurman. The social and professional insights that we have shared over the years have been immeasurably valuable, and I am grateful for your support in the writing of this book.

To my editors, Mary Somerville and Denise Rhoades, I want to thank you for your suggestions and grammatical corrections. You will note that I sometimes used your ideas and I sometimes did not. I'd like to say that anything that you see that I didn't change was because of the other editor, but that wouldn't be completely true. I took your advice most of the time, but sometimes I decided to go my own way. It was *very* helpful, however, when you *both* agreed on something that needed changing. It forced me to listen, and the book is better for it.

To Susan, Nanci, and Terri, thank you for guiding me through the various stages in my self-development journey.

Special Thanks to the following:

To all of the following organizations, businesses, and coaching programs, thank you for your exposure to so many amazing colleagues, speakers, and mentors.

MDRT, Dan Sullivan's *Strategic Coach*, Ron Carson's *Peak Advisors* and his book *Tested in the Trenches*, Tom Gau's *Million Dollar Producer*, and *Woodbury Financial Services*.

Thank you to so many of the other authors and gurus out there. If you see your ideas in my writing, I assure you that I would gladly acknowledge the credit that you so deserve. So many ideas have been implanted in my mind from the seeds (and sometimes saplings) that I acquired from a variety of books and from attendance at various conventions and coaching gatherings.

Lastly, thank you to all of my previous employers. Some of you deserve thanks for showing me what *to* do, and some of you were wonderful examples of what *not* to do. I am grateful for the experience either way.

You have all shaped me, and you all continue to shape me.

Thank You

About the Author

Tim Clairmont, is the CEO of Clear Financial Partners in Oregon with over twenty-five years as a financial advisor. Recognized globally, he's a top member of the Million Dollar Round Table and is frequently featured in outlets like Forbes, Business Insider, CNBC Make It, and more. He's authored books like "Passionate Ambivalence" and the Amazon Best Seller "What Should I Do with my 401k?" A regular guest on AM Northwest, his "Clear Money Talk" Podcast is available on Spotify and Apple Podcasts. In 2018, he educated over 14,000 global professionals on the merits of emotional intelligence while simultaneously being broadcast to an audience of over 70,000. The "ClearFP Clock" App by Clairmont helps organize assets and income in one easy-to-read, clear image; it's available for free. In 2017, he introduced the ClearFP Advisor Program™ to coach financial advisors worldwide on best practices.

Clairmont is now on a mission: **Teach ONE Billion People Something Smart About Money**. If you've learned from him, visit SomethingSmartAboutMoney.com and get counted. He's shaping a smarter financial world, one individual at a time.

"I was recently asked the question: "Who Am I?" As I was concurrently writing this book and reflecting on my life and everything that I am about, I came to this clarity: "I am the custodian of authenticity and integrity." I was born into this world with the purpose to live my life being real, genuine, and honest. As far back as I can remember, I have always found it completely abhorrent to tell an untruth or do a wrong.

I chose a career as a financial services professional. This is the most regulated, technical sales career you can possibly choose in this day and age. It was only natural that this book would become one of the fruits of this life.

I, however, am not unique. You see, I believe that each and every one of us was born with this same mission: to be custodians of authenticity and integrity. We cannot change others. We can influence others. We can persuade others. But, most importantly, we can be an example to others. I am asking you to BE that example. Live your life in authenticity and with integrity. Day by day, you will make our world a better place."

- Tim Clairmont